A short history
of the Netherlands

From prehistory to the
present day

The Golden Coach, a gift from the people of Amsterdam to Queen Wilhelmina on her ascension to the throne in 1898. It conveys the Royal Family to the Knights' Hall in The Hague on the third Tuesday in September when the new session of Parliament is opened.

A short history
of
the Netherlands

From prehistory to the present day

by Prof. dr. P.J.A.N. Rietbergen
Drs. G.H.J. Seegers

Translation M.E. Bennett

final editor Prof. dr. P.J.A.N. Rietbergen

BEKKING PUBLISHERS AMERSFOORT

Picture on cover: 'View of Delft'
  Johannes Vermeer
  (1632-1675)
  Mauritshuis The Hague

The Netherlands, a land of water. ▶

Design Gerdy Seegers
Printed in the Netherlands
by Casparie Almere bv

© 1992 Bekking Publishers Amersfoort
Postbus 286
3800 AG Amersfoort
The Netherlands

ISBN 90 6109 1802   NUGI 641

Contents

page

Society, economy and culture during the prehistoric period until 57 B.C.   13
    The Ice ages
    The earliest inhabitants
    The Funnel Beaker Culture and the Bell Beaker Culture
    The Bronze Age
    The Iron Age

Society, economy and culture during the period of Roman rule (57 B.C.- A.D.406)   21
    The influence of Roman culture
    Artificial waterways

Society and economy in the Germanic world   22
    The Crown and the Estates
    The Saxons, the Frisians and the Franks

Culture in the Germanic world: Paganism and conversion to Christianity   24
    The world of the Germanic gods
    Conversion to Christianity under the Frankish rulers
    Willibrord and Boniface

Society, politics, economy and culture in the Carolingian Empire (c. 650-850)   28
    The Frankish Empire expands
    From chamberlains to kings; the Carolingians
    The Emperor Charlemagne (800-814)
    The feudal system as instrument of administration
    The division of the Carolingian Empire   29
    The feudal system and large-scale landownership; a new estate: the villeins
    Trade flourishes
    The Carolingian renaissance

The raids of the Norsemen   33
    Declining prosperity. Departure of the Vikings

Society and politics after the disintegration of the Carolingian empire:
the beginning of regional sovereignty (c. 850-1350)   34
    The development of territorial principalities
    The Counts of Holland
    Floris V
    The diocese Utrecht
    The County, later Duchy of Gelderland
    The Duchy of Brabant
    Friesland

◄ *The Netherlands, land out of water.*

The economy from c. 1000 onwards   *41*
     Construction of dykes and reclamation of land
     The economy and the monasteries
     The rise of the towns
     New waterways
     The Hansa towns
     The political power of the towns

Culture; the role of the burghers in the towns   *44*
     The fine arts
     Religion in the towns

Society and politics in the Burgundian-Hapsburg Empire.
Centralization of power and authority (1350-1550)   *49*
     The situation from c. 1350 onwards
     Philip the Bold (1342-1404) and his matrimonial policy
     Philip the Good (1396-1467)
     Charles the Bold (1433-1477)
     Burgundy and Hapsburg; Philip the Fair (1478-1506)
     The Netherlands as part of an international union: Emperor Charles V (1500-1558)
     The regions and towns oppose the policy of centralization
     The States General and the Grand Council
     Society and economy; the growing importance of the towns of Holland

Culture (1350-1550) and new developments in religion   *59*
     Renaissance and humanism
     Education and literature
     Architecture, sculpture and painting
     Luther and Calvin

Society and politics after 1550; growing opposition to 'Spanish' rule   *67*
     King Philip II (1527-1598)
     Granvelle
     The League of the peers; the Prince of Orange and other nobles
     The first signs of revolt
     The compromise of the nobility
     The iconoclastic fury
     The renewed oath of allegiance to the king
     Alva and the Council of Blood

The struggle for independence; the 'Eighty Years' War' begins   *73*
     1568: The beginning of the war
     1572: The capture of Brill
     1573 and 1574: The relief of Alkmaar and Leiden
     1576: The Pacification of Ghent
     1579: The Union of Arras and the Union of Utrecht
     1581: The Act of Abjuration: The Northern Netherlands declares its independence
     1584: The assassination of William of Orange

The 'Republic of the Seven United Provinces' on its way to independence   *79*
     Prince Maurice and John van Oldenbarnevelt
     The Twelve Years' Truce (1609-1621)
     Arminians and Gomarians
     The Synod of Dort (1618-1619)
     The execution of John van Oldenbarnevelt (1619)

The Peace of Münster 1648: the end of the Eighty Years' War   *84*
     The political structure of the Republic

The economy in the Golden Age: the Republic at the centre of world trade   *89*
     Trade to the Baltic, the Strait and England
     Voyages of discovery
     Trading posts and colonization
     Establishment of the United East India Company or 'V.O.C.'
     Privateering and establishment of the West India Company 'W.I.C.'
     Surinam
     The Cape Colony
     The rise of industry
     The reclamation of land

Civilization in the Golden Age   *94*
     The Dutch Republic as a 'burgher state'
     Painting: genre pictures
     Baroque (religious) art
     Architecture: the Renaissance and 'Dutch Classicism'
     Literature: the Muider Circle
     Joost van den Vondel: the 'Prince of Poets'
     Hugo de Groot: founder of international law
     Music
     Science and education

Society and politics in the second half of the seventeenth century   *101*
     Stadhouder William II
     The first Stadhouderless period 1650-1672
     The Navigation Act. The First Anglo-Dutch War
     Stadhouder William III
     Pensionary John de Witt
     The struggle for a balance of power in Europe

Society, politics and economy in the late seventeenth century
and the eighteenth century   *107*
     The decline of industry
     The regents and the administration before 1747
     The second Stadhouderless period (1702-1747)
     The House of Orange: William IV and William V hereditary stadhouders in all provinces
     Patriots and Orangists

Culture in the late seventeenth century and the eighteenth century   *113*
    Flourishing activity is followed by consolidation
    Architecture and interior decoration
    Painting
    Literature
    Science and religion

Society and politics (1787-1815); revolt and foreign rule   *118*
    The Batavian Republic 1795-1806
    The Kingdom of Holland under Louis Napoleon 1806-1810
    The Netherlands annexed by France

Society, politics, economy and culture in the Kingdom
of the United Netherlands 1815-1839
    Reunion of the Northern and Southern Netherlands: the Constitution of 1815   *124*
    The establishment of the Belgian State: 1 October 1830
    William I, the Merchant-King: trade and industry
    Culture and religion under William I
    The abdication of William I: 1840

Society, politics and economy: towards an industrial society,
the first phase, until c. 1890   *128*
    The constitutional revisions of 1840 and 1848
    Limitation of the king's power
    Workers unite in organizations
    The first social legislation
    Emancipation of the Roman Catholics
    Denominational and Nonconformist education: the battle over the schools   *132*
    Ethical politics in relation to the colonies
    The political parties take shape

Culture in the nineteenth century: a long-forgotten chapter   *137*
    Painting. The Hague School and Vincent van Gogh
    Architecture: Cuypers and Berlage
    Literature: the 'Men of the Eighties' and the socialists

Society, politics and economy; towards an industrial society,
the second phase, c. 1890-1960   *138*
    The concept of neutrality
    Pacifism and fascism in the Netherlands between the World Wars
    The Depression of the 'thirties
    Government policy during the Depression
    Multinationals

Culture in the period between the two World Wars 143
    A new movement in the visual arts: 'The Style'
    Literature
    Music
    The mass media
    Science

Society and politics during World War II 145
    The German occupation: 1940-1945
    Persecution of the Jews
    The liberation of the Netherlands: 1944 and 1945

Society, politics and economy after 1945: reconstruction 147
    Clearing the rubble and starting again: new politics and parties
    Participation in international consultation
    The Dutch East Indies declares its independence: Indonesia is born
    The Charter of the Kingdom is granted to the former colonies in the West

Society, politics and economy after c. 1960 151
    The House of Orange
    The Delta project accomplished
    Economic boom and recession; social legislation and social problems

    Society and culture after 1960

Conclusion 156

Chronological outline 158

Family tree of the House of Orange-Nassau 160

A map of the Netherlands.

Introduction

The Netherlands as we now know it was moulded into its present shape over an immensely long period of time. Various elements were at work, both natural and artificial, including some of a political or military nature.

Long before man had ever won or lost territory by way of politics or military combat, he had experienced this at the hands of nature. There is no other European country in which nature, and especially water, has played such an important part as the Netherlands. As a result the inhabitants soon devised ways to curb natural influences. The gap separating the men who first built mounds or 'terpen' along the coast of Friesland and Groningen over two thousands years ago from the designers of the recently-completed Delta Project, is not so wide as it seems. The need to control water was always foremost in the minds of the Dutch, then as it is now.

Some of these natural elements also gave the land its attraction. Situated opposite England on the Delta formed by the rivers Rhine, Maas and Scheldt, the Netherlands has commanded the major transport routes of Western Europe for thousands of years. Therefore it is not surprising that this area has been a target of attack from all quarters since the beginning of history. The successive rulers known to us, the Romans, the Franks, the Burgundians and finally the Hapsburgs, have left their marks on the culture of the Netherlands. Many battles have been fought between the rulers of the various regions and against foreign invaders, to gain possession of the area and to defend or to expand it. This explains the curiously erratic borders in the east and the south which can be seen on a contemporary map of the Netherlands. These were formed by chance front lines at the end of the numerous wars waged over the Netherlands, when areas were divided among the warring parties in the ensuing peace treaties.

This book gives an outline of the history of the Netherlands from prehistory until about 1450. The Burgundian-Hapsburg period, up till about 1550 is described in greater detail including the history of what is now Belgium. The struggle for independence of the Northern Netherlands (the country as it is today) in the sixteenth and seventeenth centuries, is described extensively as the period spans the birth and recognition of the sovereign state of the Netherlands. This is followed by the development of the Republic in the seventeenth and eighteenth centuries and the temporary loss of independence under French rule. Finally, the history of the Netherlands is recorded as from 1813, when the present kingdom was established, until the present time.

'Giants' graves' in Drenthe. Stone-age megalith tombs of the Funnel Beaker Culture.

Society, economy and culture during the prehistorical period - till 57 B.C.

The ice ages

The landscape of the Netherlands was formed by consecutive ice-ages during a very long period which we call Prehistory because we have no written record of it. About 140,000 years ago, during the third ice age between about 200.000 and 130.000 B.C. part of the Netherlands was covered by a thick layer of ice. The ridges of hills to the north of the great rivers were formed when moraine was forced upwards by the ice.

As the icecap melted, the sea level rose during the following, 'Eemien Period', and the valleys hollowed out by glaciers between the hills filled with water. The sea level at that time was about the same as it is today, but the coastline was unrecognizable.

The ice did not reach the Netherlands during the fourth and last ice age, which lasted until about 10,000 B.C.; in that period the landscape was a desolate tundra.

The sea level began to rise again about 8000 B.C. and by 3000 B.C. there were sea walls or dunes along what is now the North-Sea coast. Nevertheless, large areas of the western Netherlands were flooded regularly so that this part of the country was almost uninhabitable at the beginning of the christian era.

The earliest inhabitants

All that we now know of the earliest inhabitants of this country stems from archeological finds. People lived on the site of the present Utrecht hills as long ago as 150,000 B.C. They hunted big game such as reindeer and gathered fruit and nuts. Their primitive tools were made of flint and included the familiar stone axes.

The formation of the icecap drove these inhabitants away, and as far as we know it was to be a long time before human beings returned to this country. When they did so, in about 9000 B.C. they probably had no permanent settlements as yet.
There are traces of what may have been a campsite for huntsmen in North Brabant. The flint tools used by these hunters were much finer than those of the earliest inhabitants. Stone axes dating from about 7000 B.C. were found in the North Sea, halfway to England, on land which later flooded over again.

These later inhabitants also lived on nuts and fruit as well as by hunting and fishing. However, new people arriving in about 5000 B.C. were farmers who probably also kept cattle. They lived close together on a number of large farms in the south of Limburg, the first people to settle permanently. They are known as 'band ceramists' because of the spiral design on their pottery. Like their hunting forbears, the 'band ceramists' still used implements made of flint. Flint mines were found in Limburg which must have been in use for over five centuries.

The Funnel Beaker Culture and the Bell Beaker Culture

Several of the burial places of prehistoric inhabitants of the Netherlands can still be seen, in addition to traces of their settlements and pottery. The graves of the Funnel Beaker Folk are particularly impressive. These megalith tombs or barrows were built of huge boulders, originally covered with sand. The Funnel Beaker Folk were farmers who kept cattle, like the inhabitants of the sea walls along the coast of the North Sea and the river-country community known as the "Vlaardinger Civilization".

Traces of the Bell Beaker Folk dating from about 2000 B.C. show that they had achieved an even higher level of civilization. Excavations have revealed that they had mastered the technique of forging, using imported copper.
The first primitive agricultural implements came into use at about this time, including the plough. The first ploughs would only draw a furrow in light soil, but they were still a great improvement on tilling the land by hand. Improved agricultural methods led to increased production, with the result that the population grew.

The Bronze Age

The period between 1900 and 750 B.C. is known as the Bronze Age of the Netherlands because utensils made of copper and bronze came into general use at that time.
This period was also marked by the start of widespread trading on an international scale. A splendid necklace of beads made of tin from Cornwall, amber from the Baltic and earthenware from Egypt, was excavated in Drenthe.

Plan of an iron-age farm in Amersfoort-Noord. (Department for administration and the environment, division archeology, Amersfoort).

Pot, c. 200 B.C., found on the iron-age settlement in Amersfoort-Noord. (Department for administration and the environment, division archeology, Amersfoort).

Funeral rites changed at the end of the Bronze Age. The dead were no longer buried but burnt, and urns containing the ashes were buried in special urnfields. Funerary gifts buried with them suggest that in this period the inhabitants of the south of the country were of Celtic origin and those of the north were of Germanic origin.

The Iron Age

Iron was used in the Netherlands from about 750 B.C. Colonists left the safety of the high sandy soil of Drenthe for the fertile sea clay of Groningen and Friesland at this time. They were cattle farmers who used the land for grazing. Because it was flooded regularly by the sea they constructed mounds on which they built their farmsteads. This was the earliest form of defence against the encroaching sea. Not satisfied with defending themselves against the water, the inhabitants of this country in later years also succeeded in restraining water and reclaiming land from the sea.

In the final centuries of the Prehistoric period, Germanic tribes from the north of Europe succeeded in driving the Celts ever further to the south. At the beginning of the period staved by written records, the present Netherlands was populated mainly by Germanic tribes such as the Frisians in the north and the Batavians in the country bordering the great rivers.

Schoolroom print illustrating village life during the earliest period of the Netherlands history. Made by J.H. Isings at the beginning of the 20th century, it appealed strongly to the imagination, awakening a sense of history in the children. ▶

Gaius Julius Caesar, Roman general and statesman who added western Europe - as far as the Rhine - to the Roman Empire. As a result, the southern part of the present Netherlands was also drawn into the influence of Roman culture.

Charred bones and some beads from a necklace; remains found on a cremation funeral site dating from c. AD 200 in Amersfoort-Noord. (Department for administration and the environment, division archeology, Amersfoort).

Society, economy and culture during the period of Roman Rule (57 B.C. - 406 A.D.)

The first written history that mentions the Netherlands was recorded in 57 B.C. It is mainly concerned with the country at present known as Belgium. In his renowned "Commentarii de Bello Gallico", Gaius Julius Caesar describes how his legions conquered the Celtic and Germanic tribes living in the area.

The influence of Roman culture

The advent of the Romans had far-reaching consequences for the lifestyle of the native tribes. In addition to the network of roads which the Romans built when they settled permanently, they brought their culture - religion, language and everyday life- which blended with Germanic customs, in some cases supplanting these altogether.
This applied mainly to the Germanic tribes to the south of the great rivers. The Frisians who lived further north were never subjected to Roman rule although they were obliged to pay tribute for some time. This came to an end after an uprising in the year 28.

Artificial waterways

A few centuries earlier, native tribes had first built artificial barriers against the sea. Now the Romans set about constructing the first artificial waterways. Military commander Drusus ordered a dam to be built near Cleves in 12 B.C. and also a canal connecting the Old Rhine to the river Vecht. The Drusus dam, as it was later called, was to ensure sufficient depth of the northern tributaries of the Rhine. The object of the operation was to improve the passage to the northern parts of the Netherlands which had not yet been conquered.
A military commander named Corbulo ordered a canal to be built in about 50 A.D. to join the mouths of the rivers Maas and Rhine. But in the following centuries the water again defeated the inhabitants. The whole western part of the Netherlands became an almost uninhabitable peat bog which was inundated regularly by the sea. At the beginning of the era the land in the river basins around the mouths of the Rhine and Maas was quite densely populated. But by 300 the area was practically deserted.
This decline was also linked with the decline of Roman power and authority by this time. Efficient administrative units had been formed by dividing the area into two provinces, subdivided into 'civitates' with civic centres. But these disappeared as the strong central government of the Roman Empire disintegrated. The military commanders in Rome, continually contesting for dominion during the third century, had little thought for what went on in the outposts of the empire. The result was that the northern borders became vulnerable to attack, mainly from Germanic tribes.

According to tradition, Roman rule in the Netherlands finally came to an end in 406, when the Romans were forced to surrender the series of forts they had constructed to reinforce the natural boundary formed by the Rhine.

Society and economy in the Germanic world

A great deal of the cultural influence of the Romans also disappeared when they withdrew from these parts and Germanic culture took its place. Germanic society was rather more primitive than Roman civilization, as it was based on agricultural communities. The land was divided into shires headed by a sheriff of the tribunal and an officer of the king. From the sixth century onwards these offices were usually held by one person.

During the third century, several small Germanic tribes had joined forces to form larger groups. In the course of time two main groups emerged: the Saxons and the Franks. However, the Frisians were also able to hold their ground in the north.

The Crown and the Estates

Germanic kingdoms and their form of kingship bore no resemblance to the institutions of the same name in our day and age. The Germanic kingdom was not lasting, either in time or place. Kings were chosen at a tribal meeting of free and able-bodied men. Sometimes kingship was the prerogative of members of a particular family, but even so it existed by the grace of the people. The main concern of the king was to keep in touch with world affairs involving the worlds of both gods and men. In time of war he usually led the army, though others were sometimes chosen for this task. He had no say in internal affairs such as the local administration of justice. These were dealt with by the community concerned.

Socially, the Germanic peoples were divided into four estates; the nobility (not hereditary among the Franks), the thanes, the freemen and the serfs. Only the men in the two upper estates had the right to take part in tribal meetings, which were not often convened.

The Saxons, the Frisians and the Franks

The Germanic Saxons lived mainly in the east of the Netherlands. But the centre of their administration lay east of the great Dutch rivers, in what is now Germany.

The Frisians were descendants of the colonists who had left the barren sandy soil of Drenthe and they had survived on their mounds for centuries. They were already engaged in extensive trading during the Roman period, bartering their own produce including cattle, hides and wool in exchange for luxuries, or occasionally for money. In this way the mound dwellers of the fourth and fifth centuries had achieved a high standard of civilization in comparison with the inhabitants of the rest of the country. They were able to expand and populate the land southwards as far as the great rivers, even reaching Flanders along the coast. They traded the so-called Frisian cloth across the whole of northwestern Europe, but there is some doubt as to whether this cloth was made in Friesland, or in Flanders.

The Franks who had settled to the south of the great rivers had conquered extensive territories during the centuries following the withdrawal of the Romans. Clovis I, of the Merovingian dynasty and king of the Franks from 481-511, waged numerous wars to gain dominion over the whole of Gaul, known to us today as France and northern Italy. After his death, the kingdom of the Franks was divided among his four sons who were expected to co-operate closely. Theodoric I was king of that part of the realm which included the southern Netherlands, called

Austrasia. Although still a part of the Frankish kingdom, the nobles of this area became increasingly independent. This applied mainly to the master of the royal household or chamberlain. From the seventh century onwards, these chamberlains held the actual power in the Frankish kingdom.

Plaque on the south wall of the Dom showing Roman and medieval buildings on the Dom Square. (Public record office, Utrecht).

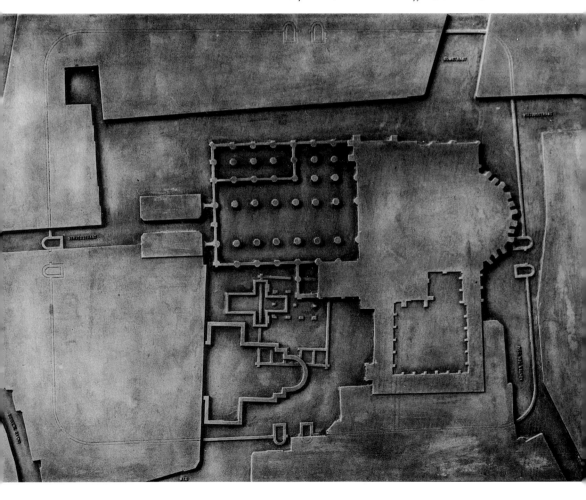

Culture in the Germanic world: Paganism and conversion to Christianity

The world of the Germanic gods

Germanic people believed in animism. They created an imaginary world from everyday experiences and peopled it with all-powerful gods. The mightiest of these was Wodan, victor in battle and forefather of all royal families.

Another powerful god was Donar, who governed the clouds and the rain, the thunder and the lightning; these powers made him very important to the farming community.

There was also Freya, the goddess of love and fertility. These and numerous other deities influenced the little things of everyday life for better or worse.

The gods were worshipped in nature, at places which were awe-inspiring in themselves, for instance by a great old tree, or on a hilltop. Sacrifices were made on an altar within an enclosure, and tribal meetings were held at the same places, giving them a hallowed atmosphere.

Conversion to Christianity under the Frankish rulers

Christianity already had some following in these parts in the fourth century. There is a record stating that Gervase, bishop of Tongeren, took part in the synods of bishops in 343 and 359. The same Gervase later removed his see from Tongeren to Maastricht. According to legend he lies buried where the church of St. Gervase still stands today.

But the real breakthrough for Christianity came with the baptism of the Frankish king Clovis I at the beginning of the sixth century. There is a legend that he pledged himself to God in the heat of battle. Obviously, this baptism also had a political

background. There were many Christians in the towns and villages of the Frankish empire, and their episcopal organization was a desirable source of power and authority to the king.

With the aid of the Frankish rulers, conversion to Christianity to the south of the great rivers was almost complete by 700, but the Germanic religion was still observed in the north.

There, the Frisians persisted obstinately in their ancestral beliefs although a small Christian church was established at Utrecht in 630. It is possible that they mistrusted the missionaries who came to convert them with the support of the Frankish rulers. It was only when Anglo-Saxon preachers from overseas visited the Frisians that their conversion took hold.

The first of these preachers was bishop Wilfred. Driven ashore on the Frisian coast while on his way to Rome, Wilfred was made welcome by king Aldgillis. He was able to preach the gospel in Friesland during the entire winter of 678.

Willibrord and Boniface

In 695 pope Sergius I consecrated the Anglo-Saxon monk Willibrord bishop of the Frisians, at that time under Frankish rule. Willibrord took up residence in the old mission post at Utrecht where he founded the churches of Saint Martin and Saint Salvator. However, Willibrord was obliged to withdraw from Utrecht when the Frisian king Radboud drove out the Franks in 714.

After successful mission work in Germany, the monk Boniface wanted to prove his worth with the Frisians in his old age. Boniface was not prepared to bring the gospel to Friesland until Willibrord had returned to Utrecht. This took place in 734, the year in which Friesland was finally annexed to the Frankish empire after being defeated by Charles Martel. But there were Frisians who did not welcome Boniface's efforts. The murder of Boniface near Dokkum in 754 showed that paganism in Friesland was still a strong force in the middle of the eighth century.

Schoolroom print by J.H. Isings showing a mission of the first Christian preachers to the northern Netherlands. ▶

The church of St. Salvator, Utrecht, showing the church as it was c. 1580. The building adjoining the tower was the Dom school. ▼

Society, politics, economy and culture in the Carolingian Empire (c. 650-850)

The Frankish empire expands

For centuries the great rivers had served as a natural boundary with the domains to the south, first the Roman empire and later the Frankish empire. The Romans had built a number of military forts along the Rhine. At one of these - fort Levefanum - a trading centre sprang up during the seventh century called Dorestad, near the present site of Wijk bij Duurstede. This trading centre was of great importance to both the Frisians and the Franks as it dominated trade in the whole of northwestern Europe, including the supply of silver from Russia and Persia so essential to the western-European economy. Fierce fighting ensued over this place.

In 689 the Frankish chamberlain Pepin II defeated the Frisian king Radboud at Dorestad. After Pepin's death, Radboud succeeded in recovering the ground won by the Franks. Meanwhile, the rule of the Frisian kings was drawing to a close. In 734 the Frisian military commander Bubo was defeated by the Frankish chamberlain Charles Martel, extending the Frankish kingdom to the 'Lauwers' and the North Sea.

From chamberlains to kings: the Carolingians

Charles's son Pepin III proclaimed himself king of the Franks after deposing the last Merovingian ruler. He was annointed by the missionary Boniface to demonstrate that his kingship was of a different nature to that of the primitive Germanic rulers. In this way the Crown gained a new dignity derived from the Old Testament, raising it above the simple authority of former days.

The Emperor Charlemagne (800-814)

The first Carolingian to be annointed king, Pepin III, died in 768. He was succeeded by his two sons, one of whom died only three years later. Charles, the remaining son, then became the absolute monarch, known to the people as Charlemagne. He campaigned relentlessly against the Saxons. Following a decisive victory over them in 785, his rule was accepted in these parts.

Charlemagne saw himself as the lawful successor to the Roman emperors. For this reason he went to Rome to be crowned by the pope in 800.
The empire had no particular capital city.

Equestrian statue of the Emperor Charlemagne (800-816).

Charlemagne often held court at Aachen. He paid regular visits to the outposts of his territories and he sometimes stayed in the Netherlands, where he had a castle at Nijmegen.

The realm of Charlemagne was administered by civil servants, or counts in charge of the counties. The names of several of these counties have survived in the present Netherlands, as in Twente, Batua (Betuwe), Gooi and Brabant. The main task of Carolingian counts was to administer justice at the head of a tribunal of freemen.

The feudal system as instrument of administration

The feudal system developed during the rule of the Frankish kings. The rulers surrounded themselves with loyal followers, entrusting them with various administrative and military duties. High - ranking civil servants were rewarded with land and certain privileges. Those who joined in their campaigns were often granted land in fee, but those who lost their land to a Frankish king in combat were also allowed to hold their land in fee. In exchange they had to acknowledge Frankish sovereignty. The invasions of the Vikings between 800 and 1000 certainly caused many to entrust or enfief - hence fee and 'feudal' - their land to powerful authorities, their ruler or the church, in order to receive protection in exchange.

The division of the Carolingian empire

Charlemagne was succeeded by his son Louis the Pious on his death in 814. The empire was divided among Louis' three sons at the Treaty of Verdun in 843. Lothair inherited the central part, including the region later to be the Netherlands and with it the emperor's crown.
On the death of Lothair in 855, the central empire was again divided, once more into three parts, with the Netherlands in the northernmost part, called Lorraine. Following various other divisions and annexations to East and West Frankland, Henry I, king of Germany, succeeded in subjecting Lorraine, or the Netherlands, to his rule in 925. Officially it was to remain part of the Holy Roman Empire until 1648, but actual power soon lay elsewhere.

The feudal system and large-scale landownership; a new class: the villeins

Agriculture and livestock were still the main sources of livelihood in Carolingian times. But the rise of feudalism brought considerable changes in economic and social organization. Previously rare, large-scale landownership became the rule now, especially in the south. This resulted in a new class of people, the villeins, who had a piece of land for their own use, but who were also obliged to cultivate the land belonging to their landlord. The disappearance of a money-based economy also played a part in this reversion to an agricultural economy. Payments were usually made in kind and by means of personal services.

Trade flourishes

In addition to agriculture, trading between the towns began to play a greater part in providing a livelihood. As boundaries shifted to the north under Carolingian rule, this led to brisk trading in northwest Europe during the eighth and ninth centuries with the Frisians playing a leading part. The old trading centre of Dorestad grew during this period to become the foremost Frisian trading town. During the ninth century this flourishing trading centre suffered many attacks at the hands of Nordic marauders. However, it is likely that the harbour was already falling into disuse due to the shifting bed of the Rhine. Other important trading towns were Medemblik and Stavoren.

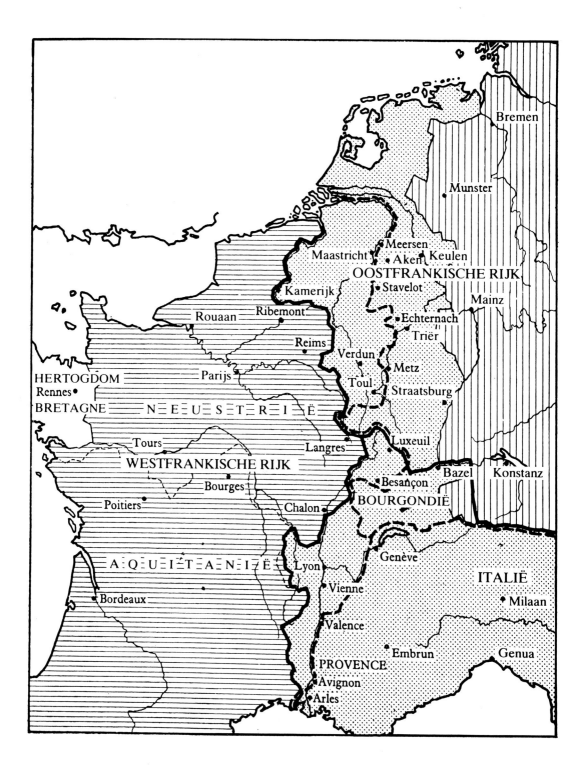

Bremen

Munster

Meersen

Maastricht Aken Keulen

OOSTFRANKISCHE RIJK

Stavelot Mainz

Kamerijk

Rouaan Ribemont

Echternach

Reims Trïer

Verdun

Parijs Metz

Toul Straatsburg

HERTOGDOM

Rennes

BRETAGNE N E U S T R I Ë

Tours Langres Luxeuil

WESTFRANKISCHE RIJK Bazel Konstanz

Bourges Besançon

Poitiers Chalon BOURGONDIË

Genève

A Q U I T A N I Ë Lyon ITALIË

Vienne Milaan

Bordeaux

Valence

Embrun Genua

PROVENCE

Avignon

Arles

Carolingian renaissance

There was a revival of interest in ancient Roman and Greek elements of culture during the ninth and tenth centuries. This Carolingian 'renaissance' was concentrated in the monastries and manifested itself mainly in the fields of philosophy, literature and art. Many a classic was preserved for posterity during the Carolingian period by the monks' zeal. Always eager to learn, it is said that Charlemagne studied Latin late in life. He also promoted education. The church was to provide this education on a classical basis. The subjects that were taught were called the seven liberal arts. The 'trivium' included grammar, rhetoric and logic for younger pupils, and the 'quadrivium', for more advanced pupils, consisted of geometry, astronomy, arithmetic and music. In reality this education was reserved for a select few, mainly prospective clergy and members of the nobility. Lessons were given in monastery and chapter schools. The schools in Utrecht attached to the churches of Saint Martin and Saint Salvator became renowned. Future clergy from the whole of the northern Frankish empire were sent to these schools.

Charlemagne also stimulated education in music. He founded a choir school at Metz, and by introducing the Gregorian plainsong hymnal he succeeded in persuading the clergy to introduce hymn-singing during church services.

Division of the Carolingian Empire in the Treaty of Verdun, of 843

the western empire of Charles the Bold

the central empire of Lothair

the eastern empire of Louis the German .

Replica of a Viking longship with large square sails.

Reconstruction of a more robust ship found near Gokstadt, used by the Vikings for long voyages.

Reconstruction of a Viking ship, found near Oseberg in Norway. This elegant ship was probably used for short journeys only.

The raids of the Norsemen

The name Norseman or Viking does not denote any specific ethnic group; they were the names given to inhabitants of the Nordic countries we now know as Denmark, Norway and Sweden, between about 800 and 1050. The Vikings went down in history as plunderers and pirates, raiding most of the European coastal areas in their well-equipped longboats during the summer months and returning home with stolen treasure.

Most of the Vikings who raided the Netherlands came from Denmark. They attacked these parts regularly, especially after the death of Charlemagne, as central authority weakened in the Frankish empire due to its repeated division among the many heirs.

The Vikings concentrated their raids on churches and monasteries - the only source of real riches, with treasure-houses containing gold, silver and precious stones. The population of this country suffered the worst attacks between 879 and 882, when the Vikings set up fortified camps at various places from which they launched their forays. Their leader Godfried the Pirate was even appointed governor of Friesland after being baptized. He was not alone in conforming. During the first decades, the Vikings carried out their forays in summer only. Later they also took to spending the winter in the regions they plundered. In an attempt to limit the power of these marauders, land was sometimes granted to their leaders in fee by the Carolingian ruler. In exchange, the Vikings who collaborated were obliged to assist the local ruler in his struggle against other Vikings. A Viking called Harald acquired 'a princedom' on the island of Walcheren in this way in 841; a few years later a relation of his called Rorik became ruler over the area which included Dorestad.

Declining prosperity. Departure of the Vikings

The harvest failed in 892, resulting in a severe shortage of food. This was the signal for the Vikings to withdraw from the Netherlands and to turn their attention to England for their forays; after this only isolated attacks were made on this country. The bishops of Utrecht, who had taken refuge elsewhere in the middle of the ninth century, returned to Utrecht in 920.

The last raids were carried out between 1006 and 1007 when Tiel was one of the places to be plundered. From this time onwards the Vikings lost their terror as most of them had already been converted to Christianity.

Society and politics after the disintegration of the Carolingian empire: the beginning of regional sovereignty (c. 850-1350)

The development of territorial principalities

The division that finally resulted in the provinces of the present Netherlands was already roughly outlined in the year 1000. After the incorporation of the Netherlands in Lorraine in 855 and in the German Empire in 925, a number of larger principalities was formed by the conquest or merging of smaller counties. Most of these were governed by counts. Though they had been little more than royal civil servants in Carolingian times, they had gradually acquired power and land so that now they were largely independent governors, subject in name only to the rulers of the German Empire.

The Counts of Holland

The County of Holland was the first to develop. The heart of this region was Kennemara or Kennemerland, which was granted in fee to the Viking Rorik in 862. Another Viking, Gerulf, who was Count of Kennemerland in 885, became the forefather of the Counts of Holland. A century later one of his descendants, Dirk II, was granted the entire region between the rivers Maas and Vlie under his administration, in recognition of his support of the election of the German King Otto II.
Count Dirk III began to levy a toll from the merchant ships sailing in and out of the Maas estuary. A punitive expedition sent against him by the Duke of Lower Lorraine and the Bishop of Utrecht ended in failure as the troops floundered in the sodden marshlands surrounding Vlaardingen. This incident illustrates the independence of the region as a political and administrative entity.

The name Holland first appeared in a deed dated 1083, in which Dirk V confirmed the property of the abbey of Egmond and referred to himself as "Count of Holland". The territory of the Counts of Holland was extended considerably in the course of the centuries, mainly by conquests over their neighbours. For instance, Flanders was under continual attack for the possession of Zeeland to the east of the Scheldt, which eventually met with success. Zeeland to the west of the Scheldt was governed jointly by Brabant and Holland; William I is duly referred to in records as Count of Holland and Zeeland.

The Frisians were also attacked for the possession of West- Friesland. The West-Frisians in their turn regularly raided and plundered Holland as they became isolated from their native country. This happened when the straits connecting the North Sea with the Almere grew steadily wider to form the Zuiderzee, now known as the IJsselmeer. This part of Friesland did not become subordinate to Holland until 1289.

Floris V

Floris V of Holland was only two years old when his father William II died in 1256, and a long struggle for the regency ensued which weakened the authority of the Count for a time. When Floris came of age, it soon became clear that he was anxious to extend his powers. The Kennemer peasants revolted against the Count in 1274 with the support of Gijsbrecht van Amstel, a nobleman of the Sticht Utrecht who rebelled against the power of Floris. The dispute was settled in their favour, Floris being obliged to grant the peasants a number of privileges. After this he could do no wrong with them and he was known as "God of the churls". But his relations with the nobles did not improve. Floris sometimes confiscated their possessions to punish them, only returning them in fee in exchange for their oath of fealty. Van Amstel and the nobles of Woerden were treated in this way. Some of them took revenge in 1296 by imprisoning Floris in the castle of Muiden. When a group of peasants tried to free him, they murdered him.

Muiden Castle in winter, by Jan Beerstraten (1622-1666). Floris V was imprisoned here in 1296 and subsequently murdered. Muiden Castle was host to one of the leading cultural circles of Holland in the 17th century.

The struggle between Floris V and the nobles was a sign of the times. In other principalities too, a feudal aristocracy had grown overmighty as the system expanded, and there was an increasing tendency to oppose the authority of the ruler. As a result the ruler often joined forces with representatives of towns growing in importance economically and consequently politically. As the nobles fought amongst themselves as well, they often appealed for help to the towns which liked to fish in troubled water if there was something to be gained.

The disputes between the 'Hoeksen' (Hooks) and 'Kabeljauwsen' (Cods) two 'parties' in the county of Holland, were notorious. They arose over the struggle for

succession in the counties Holland, Zeeland and Hainault, which had formed a personal union. In 1345 William IV was killed during a campaign to subdue Friesland. In the absence of a son and heir, the German Emperor granted the three counties to his own wife Margaretha, sister of William IV. Her son William, still a minor, was appointed as heir.

In the following years however, mother and son disputed each other's right of succession; William had persuaded some of the nobles and a number of towns to take his side in the Kabeljauwse 'party'. Margaretha formed the Hoeksen 'party' with the support of other nobles. William finally gained possession of Holland and Zeeland in 1354, while Margaretha retained Hainault. At the end of the fourteenth century the feud between 'Hoeksen' and 'Kabeljauwse' flared up once again over inheritance. But the independence enjoyed by the county was coming to an end; a larger administrative body was beginning to form in the duchy of Burgundy in which the principalities of Hainault, Holland and Zeeland were incorporated.

The diocese of Utrecht

Whereas Holland was a secular principality, the Sticht Utrecht was administered by a religious leader, the bishop. For instance, Ansfried, Bishop of Utrecht from 995-1010 had frequently fought at the King's side before his appointment to The Sticht. As the succession to a diocese could never be hereditary, the King was always able to appoint a figure who would be loyal to him.

In their struggle against the growing power of their vassals or thanes, such as the Counts of Holland, the German Kings sought added support by giving secular power to the leading clergy. They often gave extensive property to the bishops appointed by them,

to assure themselves of their undying loyalty.

The Bishop of Utrecht had first received extensive estates and lands from Charlemagne; after 950 the bishops were also granted the authority of a count by the German emperors and played their part in governing the land. The dignity of the see turned into a position of great power, coveted by nobles and royal relations. Bishops were rarely clergy with a true mission.

In 1024 Bishop Adalbold was presented with the entire County of Drenthe by the German King. In the following years this territory was extended further. The areas in which the bishops wielded secular power were known as 'Lower' Sticht (roughly the Province of Utrecht today) and 'Upper' Sticht (now Overijssel and Drenthe).

The so-called Investiture Controversy broke out in the eleventh century between the Pope and the Emperor, over the right of the Emperor to appoint the senior clergy, including the bishops. At the Concordat of Worms in 1122 it was decided that in future, bishops were to be elected by the canons, the high-ranking clergy serving the cathedral of the diocese. In Utrecht they were the canons of the five chapters there, led by the dean of the Dom, the Cathedral. Now that the Emperor had lost his hold on Utrecht, the rulers of small neighbouring states such as Holland and Brabant tried to gain influence over the secular government of The Sticht. When the see of Utrecht became vacant they were known to push their own relations forward as candidates.

The Dom Cathedral, Utrecht. Building was begun in 1321 and completed in 1382. The illustration is an early 19th-century colour litho.

Consequently, warlike feuds between parties supporting different candidates frequently rent The Sticht. In 1196 there were two candidates. One was the uncle of the Count of Holland, the other a protégé of the Count of Gelderland. In their zeal to acquire the coveted see for their own candidates, both parties occupied a part of The Sticht. Peace was not restored until a neutral figure was appointed after both candidates had died.
Naturally the inhabitants of both town and country of The Sticht were troubled by these disputes.

Candidates for the see needed so much money for their election campaigns and to defend their position, that they often resorted to pawning their (future) property. In 1331 Bishop Jan van Diest was powerless to intervene when Holland and Gelderland divided The Sticht into spheres of influence between them, because he had pledged almost all his possessions as collateral. Occasionally the bishop was a strong figure, like Jan van Arkel who succeeded in reuniting The Sticht under the episcopal administration in 1362. But such men were unable to prevent the principality from being drawn into the influence of another increasingly powerful neighbour, eventually to become, like Holland, part of a greater political entity.

The County, later Duchy of Gelderland

The County of Gelderland, which became a Duchy in 1339, was late to develop. It did not begin to resemble the Province of Gelderland as it is today until the end of the twelfth century.

Gelderland was not spared the feuds among its aristocracy as already described concerning Holland and Utrecht. In Gelderland too these feuds were often the result of a dispute over the succession. In 1343 the families of the Lords of Hekeren

and Bronkhorst interfered with the guardianship of the heir -a minor- to the first Duke of Gelderland, Reynold II. From 1350 on they also joined in the feud between Reynold III and his brother Edward, until both rivals died in 1371. For many years the 'parties' of the Hekerens and the Bronkhorsts continued to wage wars, resembling the struggle between the Hoekse and Kabeljauwse groups in Holland.
Like other minor states, Gelderland sometimes attacked its neighbours. The most powerful of these was the Duchy of Brabant.

The Duchy of Brabant

Brabant, with its fertile lands and wealthy towns, was a major power in this region. It had some influence in the County of Holland during the thirteenth century. Henry II, Duke of Brabant had supported the election of William II, Count of Holland, to be crowned King of the Romans within the German Empire in 1248. William, who was ambitious, tried to use his position to gain possession of Flanders. He was prevented from accomplishing this as he was killed during a campaign against the West-Frisians in 1256.

Brabant also played a leading part in European politics for many years. The Dukes of Brabant were important figures in the German Empire itself. In the struggle between the Staufen and the Welfen, parties for the imperial crown (1198-1214), they supported one or other of these in turn, depending on what they were offered in return. This brought them into conflict with England and France, which supported the Welfian and Staufian candidates for the throne respectively.

Brabant had its golden age between 1267 and 1355. The prospects for Brabant had not been favorable when Henry III died in 1261; a struggle for the succession, like those in other parts of the Netherlands, seemed inevitable. On his death, Henry III's sons were underage, and his eldest son and heir, Henry, was mentally and physically handicapped. Henry III's widow succeeded in becoming his guardian and she permitted co-guardianship to her most influential neighbour Count Otto II of Gelderland and the Prince-Bishop of Liège. This arrangement, which was made with the support of the clergy, the aristocracy and the towns, gathered in the so-called *States of Brabant*, averted a dynastic crisis and assured peace in the land.

When Henry IV came of age he renounced his rights at an assembly of the States, after which he entered a monastery. His younger brother John succeeded him to become one of the most colourful dukes in the history of Brabant.

When Duke John III died in 1355 without male issue, he was succeeded by his daughter Johanna. A charter was drawn up on this occasion to specify the rights of the towns. It was called 'The Joyous Entry'. It set the seal on a political development in which Brabant led the way for other regions by defining the relations between the lord and his subjects, a statement in writing of the rights and obligations of both. The Joyous Entry was a guarantee to the towns that the duke would not start a costly war without their permission. It also enabled them to make sure that revenues were spent wisely.

Friesland

In contrast with the states described above, Friesland had no dynasty of its own. A series of lords from the House of Bruno, from Brunswick, were in power there during the eleventh century. Little is known about them, but their coins struck in various Frisian towns, have been found as far away as Russia.

The population of Friesland lived in several small counties such as Staveren - which had already been granted to the Bishop of Utrecht in 1077 - and Oostergo and Westergo, corresponding respectively to the east and west of Friesland as it is today. When Egbert II, the last of the Bruno's, rebelled against the German Emperor Henry IV, Oostergo and Westergo were taken away from him and also granted to the Bishop of Utrecht in fee in 1089. However, the Bishops of Utrecht and the Counts of Holland tried to gain control of the Frisian counties during the twelfth century. Emperor Frederick Barbarossa eventually decided to let Utrecht and Holland govern Friesland jointly.

William, the brother of the ruling Count of Holland, was appointed Count of Friesland in 1197 but he did not have long to establish his authority. On the death of his brother in 1203 he also became Count of Holland. In the absence of their lord the Frisians no longer felt accountable to him. They were free once more. Feuds now broke out between several great landowning families who attacked each other from their strongholds with small armies. This strife, comparable to that in other principalities, was made worse by the influence of the mighty monasteries of the Cistercian and Norbertine orders. The majority of monks in Frisian monasteries during the thirteenth century were lay brothers who had not taken vows. They sometimes grew overmighty in which case monastic discipline slackened. In about 1340 a feud broke out between the monasteries of Bloemkamp and Lidlum. Bloemkamp was a Cistercian monastery. The monks belonging to this order wore grey habits and were called greyfriars or 'Schieringers'. This is also the origin of the name of the island Schiermonnikoog which belonged to the monastery at that time. The monks of Lidlum belonged to the Norbertine order. Because their wealth was mainly based on cattle, they were known as 'Vetkopers' (butter-boxes). Therefore Frisian party-feuds were called after the struggle between the 'Schieringers' and the 'Vetkopers'.

This struggle flared up continually during the second half of the fourteenth and the whole of the fifteenth century, when peasants and commoners, clergy and laymen and the various noble families all fought among themselves. The Schieringers, who lived in Oostergo were usually in favour of independence for Friesland; the Vetkopers, who lived mainly in what is now the Province of Friesland, were inclined to join forces with Holland. These feuds led to plundering, raiding and arson, causing great harm to the Frisian people in the absence of a higher authority to control them.

Occasionally one of the Counts of Holland attempted to claim the rights of Holland to Friesland, still valid in name.
William IV raised a large army in 1345 in order to subdue the Frisians. William was killed and his army was defeated soundly during the ensuing Battle of Warns, a village in the southwest of Friesland.

Later attempts to establish the authority of the Counts in Friesland at the end of the fourteenth century also met with failure. The Frisians did not finally lose their freedom until the end of the fifteenth century, and then not to the Counts of Holland but to the German Emperor. He subjected rebellious Friesland to his own direct rule by appointing a 'Stadhouder' or Lieutenant.

Memorial to the 'Battle of Warns', 1345. The Frisians defeated the Dutch. The epitaph reads "Death rather than bondage".

The economy from c. 1000 onwards

Construction of dykes and reclamation of land

Peace returned when the Vikings ceased their raids and the population began to increase. Wasteland was cultivated to meet the need for more land by the people who still lived mainly by agriculture and cattle farming. Low-lying areas were drained and protected by dykes, and marshland was reclaimed. The farmers of Holland and Friesland became so skilled at this work that, in 1113, the Archbishop of Hamburg offered them land in Saxony for reclamation. In this way colonists from Holland and Friesland helped to populate eastern Germany.

In addition to the need for more land, the rising sea level also necessitated the construction of dykes. In the thirteenth century seawater poured into the land via the Almere. The construction of sea dykes, such as the dyke between Harlingen and Stavoren, became a dire necessity to save the land from regular inundation and siltation.

Organizations called water boards were formed to ensure that the dykes were kept in good repair and to regulate the water level in low-lying areas. This was one example of a general tendency to order and regulate everyday life. The same tendency was also noticeable in the church, where episcopal re-organizaton took place in the dioceses involving the appointment of archdeacons and suffragan bishops. At a lower level, large parishes were split up into numerous smaller ones, with boundaries corresponding roughly to those of a village in order to increase the hold on churchlife and the community.

The economy and the monasteries

The first monasteries in this country were often established by the richest and most powerful figures in society, the overlord and the nobles. For instance, Rijnsburg Abbey was founded by Countess Petronella of Holland in 1133.
The monasteries were large communities of sometimes as many as a thousand people. Most of them were in the country, concerned mainly with the management of their often extensive lands; they instigated a great deal of useful work. The monks were foremost in constructing dykes and pioneers in reclaiming land and cultivating wasteland.
Smaller monasteries arose in the fourteenth century, usually with a more contemplative background. They were not situated in the country, but in the towns which had been founded during the preceding centuries.

The rise of the towns

The rise of the towns in the eleventh and twelfth centuries, partly due to the growing population, was also influenced by the slow but steady increase in trade and industry in those times.
Before the turn of the millenium, the Germanic tribes were mostly dependent on the land for a living, but they were also active in trade; they had several flourishing trading centres such as Dorestad, described in an earlier chapter. But at that time there was no production of goods specifically for trading purposes on a regional level. During the eleventh and twelfth centuries Europe renewed and stepped up its contacts with promising sources overseas. Trade with the Near East, so rich in luxury goods, was resumed after the first crusade in 1096. England produced huge quantities of wool

for the textile industry, and trade with this country increased considerably after the duke of Normandy had conquered it in 1066.

Trade and industry were concentrated in the towns, which also drew produce from the surrounding rural areas at the weekly markets and annual fairs. Supplies of wood and other provisions had to be brought into these trading centres for the daily needs of the townspeople who could not produce these for themselves.

New waterways

As trade increased, and the range of products grew in number and volume, larger ships were needed which could not navigate the old inland waterways. Other navigation routes came into use, including one over the North Sea through the Sound. This meant that new markets came within reach, such as the rich Baltic ports, where there was a plentiful supply of grain and wood for shipment to the Netherlands. The old trading centres of Tiel and Utrecht, which depended on the great rivers to transport their merchandise, could no longer compete with the seaports in the north such as Stavoren, Leeuwarden, Groningen, Dokkum and Bolsward. From these ports merchant shipping set out for Germany and England.

The Hansa towns

Merchants also navigated the Sound from towns on the Zuider Zee and the River IJssel, including Harderwijk, Elburg, Deventer and Kampen; this was known as around-country shipping. Many of these towns joined the Hanseatic League, a merchant guild which united numerous German and Dutch trading towns to defend their interests jointly.

The independent approach of these towns in economic affairs was partly due to the freedom enjoyed by town councils in decision making. This was one of the privileges laid down in the town charter, granted by the overlords to the towns in their territory. In return they hoped for financial support in their wars, from the ever richer and more powerful merchants. One of the earliest examples of a charter of this kind dates from 1185, when Duke Henry I of Brabant granted a number of privileges to s'Hertogenbosch. Later charters often followed this early example. The privileges granted to Haarlem and s'Gravenzande in 1245 by Count William II of Holland were based on those of "Den Bosch".

The political power of the towns

The wealth and the independence afforded by their privileges enabled the towns to assume political power along with the ruler, the aristocracy and the church. In the fifteenth century many of the towns operated as virtually independent communities, also forming strong political factions in the many party feuds. They often intervened in questions of succession as they knew by experience how damaging the resulting feuds could be; wars cost money and hampered trade. Town councils no longer submitted to taxation or the obligation to take part in a war without question; like the aristocracy, they wanted to be consulted first. This led to consultation in all the principalities, between representatives of the clergy, the aristocracy and the towns, known as the assembly of the Estates. In Brabant Duke John II issued the charter of Kortenberg in 1312. This charter called for a council of fourteen members to be formed comprising four members of the aristocracy, and ten representatives from the towns.

The right of this council to have a say in certain matters of state mentioned above was acknowledged and confirmed in the 'Joyous Entry'.

In the Sticht, the burghers of the city of
Utrecht already had some say in the election
of a bishop in the twelfth century. The
assembly of the Estates in which the towns
and the aristocracy (each representing its
own 'estate') formed a union, originated in
Utrecht in the 'Charter for the Land' written
in 1375 by Bishop Arnold of Horn. He was
obliged to make concessions in this
document after the unfortunate outcome of
a war against Holland and Gelderland.
The fear that the question of succession
would also stir up trouble in Gelderland,
prompted the aristocracy and the towns to
join forces. Reynold IV acknowledged the
rights of the 'States of Gelderland' in 1419.
United in a personal union under Count
William V, in the counties of Holland,
Zeeland and Hainault, the Estates jointly
drew up new regulations in 1362 to give
themselves considerable influence.

*The 'Kamperpoort', remains of past wealth and
power of the Hansa town, Kampen.*

43

Culture: the role of the burghers in the towns

The rise of the towns also had other effects. About the year 1000 cultural activity was mainly confined to the circles of the aristocracy and the clergy, particularly in the monasteries. The surviving Greek and Latin classics were preserved and copied here, and the first chronicles recording contemporary life were written by Emo and Menko in the thirteenth century. Both Emo and Menko later became Abbot of the Bloemhof monastery in Groningen. Latin was the language used for writing in the monasteries.
The result of the rise of towns and the growing wealth of the burghers was that the Dutch vernacular was used increasingly in writing, from the thirteenth century onwards. The Verse Chronicle of Melis Stoke - soon after 1300- and the works of Jacob van Maerlant are good examples of this.

In architecture, the transition to an urban culture was particularly noticeable in the churches.
The Romanesque style of architecture, particularly in the north, was mainly the art of the rural areas; buildings with massive walls, windows and doors with rounded arches and the simple saddle-roof towers so characteristic of Groningen and Friesland. Examples of this Romanesque architecture can still be found today in some of the villages in the northern provinces.

The surviving Romanesque architecture in the south of the country, represented by the lovely churches of St. Gervase and Our Lady in Maastricht, is more monumental and belongs to another stream known as the Maasland style. Famed for its wrought-iron work, this style reached its peak in the eleventh and twelfth centuries. Maastricht was the centre for the Maasland style and

magnificent reliquaries were made here in the twelfth century. Perhaps the loveliest of these is the shrine of St. Gervase which is still kept in the church of the same name.

There were craftsmen in wrought-iron at work in the north too, but they did not achieve the high standard of the south. What is left of their work consists mainly of coins and cloister seals, including that of Egmond Abbey. The oldest surviving shrine from the north was made in Utrecht in 1362.

Lighter and more elegant Gothic architecture developed in the towns during the fourteenth and fifteenth centuries, to create ever lovelier churches with tall spires and stained-glass windows.
The most famous fourteenth-century Gothic architecture in this country can be seen in Utrecht and s'Hertogenbosch. Building on the tower of the Dom church in Utrecht began in 1321. It was designed by the master builder Jan van Henegouwen and completed in 1382, 110 metres in height. The choir of this church also dates from the fourteenth century.
The magnificent cathedral of St. John in s'Hertogenbosch was also built in the fourteenth century.

The best-known example of a secular Gothic building is the Ridderzaal or Great Hall in The Hague, which was built at the end of the thirteenth century by order of Count Floris V of Holland. This hall, which has been rather overrestored, is the scene of the annual ceremony for the opening of Parliament.

The fine arts

Painting did not flourish in the Netherlands until the fifteenth century. There was some

The church of St. Gervase, Maastricht as it is today.

Reliquary of St. Gervase. One of the finest examples of 12th-century wrought-iron work in the 'Maaslands-Romanesque' style.

St. John's Cathedral, Den Bosch, an example of Gothic architecture in the 14th and 15th centuries. Detail of the central nave. ▶

miniature painting, usually illustrations to the manuscripts written in the monasteries. This form of art, in contrast with others, was not influenced by awakening cultural activity in the towns. There are some surviving examples of this art in missals made for nobles and clergy in Utrecht and Gelderland.

Monumental painting before 1350 was rare and is represented only by a few murals. There are also some rare late fourteenth-century painted panels most of which were made in Gelderland and Utrecht. They were memorial tableaux, to be placed in church near the tomb of the high-ranking person to whom they were dedicated.

Sculpture from this period is also scarce. The few remaining works are mainly monuments to nobles and high-ranking clergy, such as the memorial to Jan van Arkel in the church at Gorinchem.

Religion in the towns

In general, all the art forms of this period reflect the important part played by religion in everyday life. Until the fourteenth century the aristocracy and the clergy were still the leading patrons of the arts; but the class of wealthy burghers which had developed in the towns was gradually coming into its own. It is significant that in religion too, it was this new class which was susceptible to new trends.

The establishment of small monasteries in the towns instead of in the country was mentioned above. Many of these had their roots in the Modern Devotion, a movement started by Geert Grote of Deventer c. 1384. The object of this movement was to return to a simple way of life based on religion. Strangely, this appealed predominantly to the educated and wealthy citizens who formed religious brotherhoods, but without the obligation to take vows. These religious congregations later often joined one of the existing monastic orders, usually the Franciscans.

The Knight's Hall, The Hague. Built in the 13th-century by order of Floris V as part of the palace of the Counts of Holland.

Society and politics in the Burgundian-Hapsburg Empire. Centralization of power and authority (1350-1550)

The period from the tenth to the fourteenth century saw the formation of regional states in the Netherlands, later to become the provinces of the present kingdom. The foundation for the character of the Netherlands was laid during this period in geographic, economic, political and cultural aspects. Towards the end of this period we see the towns taking their place beside the ruler, the aristocracy and the clergy, with increasing influence in the economy and in politics. Society in the Netherlands gradually became more urban and the culture of the burghers set the tone.

The situation from 1350 onwards

About 1350 most of the future regions of the Netherlands were already established as semi-independent states. But the authority of the various dynasties had gradually dwindled due to internal conflicts and the rise of the burghers; the resulting assemblies of the Estates imposed all kinds of limits on the rulers, mainly to curb expenditure. In the late fourteenth and fifteenth centuries there were two contrasting developments. On the one hand many towns grew into robust little states going their own way; on the other hand the power over the various principalities became concentrated in one single family, that of the Dukes of Burgundy alone, who acquired it through marriages, inheritance and wars.

Philip the Bold (1342-1404) and his matrimonial policy

In 1363 the King of France gave the Duchy of Burgundy to his son Philip the Bold, who married Margaretha of Flanders, the heiress to the County of Burgundy (Franche-Comté) in 1369. On the death of his father-in-law in 1384 Philip inherited Flanders, Artois,

Nevers, Rethel and also the towns won from Brabant- Antwerp and Mechlin.
From then on the Burgundian duchy continued to extend northwards, but it lost some ground in the south, including Nevers in 1404.

Philip succeeded in arranging favourable marriages for his children. A double wedding took place in 1385, the first between his son John, later known as John the Fearless, and Margaretha of Bavaria. The second between his daughter Margaretha and the brother of Margaretha of Bavaria, William VI, who became Count of Holland, Zeeland and Hainault in 1404. He was succeeded on his death in 1417 by his daughter Jacqueline of Bavaria who was married to Duke John IV of Brabant.

Philip the Good (1396-1467)

It was Philip the Good, son of John the Fearless, who succeeded in uniting all these regions under his rule. After a fierce struggle with his cousin Jacqueline of Hainault, during which the Hoekse and Kabeljauwse disputes flared up again as bitterly as ever, a compromise was reached in 1428. This entailed that Jacqueline relinquished any real power to Philip, while keeping her titles. Neither was she free to remarry without the permission of Philip, her mother, and the assembled Estates of her regions. When, in spite of this treaty she secretly married the Zeeland noble, Frank van Borselen, she also forfeited her titles and Philip succeeded her as Count of Holland, Zeeland and Hainault.

Brabant had already come into Philip's possession in 1430 because his two cousins had died childless. In 1451 he also inherited Luxembourg with the result that, in

PHILIPS van BORGONJE.

*17th-century engraving showing Philip the Good
(1396-1467), Duke of Burgundy, Count of
Holland, Zeeland and Hainault, he also inherited
Brabant and Luxembourg.*

MARIA van BORGONJE.   MAXIMILIAAN van OOSTENRYK.

17th-century engraving: As a result of the marriage in 1477 of this couple, Maximilian of Hapsburg, Archduke of Austria and Mary of Burgundy, the interests of the Netherlands became part of the international politics of the Hapsburgs.

addition to the ancestral part of Burgundy, his empire then included the present territory of Belgium, Luxembourg and a large part of the Netherlands. Gelderland, Utrecht, Friesland and Groningen were not yet a part of it. But in 1456 Utrecht, Overijssel and Drenthe were brought into the Burgundian camp when Philip succeeded in having his bastard son David appointed Bishop of Utrecht.

Friesland stayed out of Burgundian reach for a long time. Groningen too, held on to its independence for the time being with occasional support from the Dukes of Gelderland.

These dukes became the toughest opponents of Burgundian expansion.

Charles the Bold (1433-1477)

Like his father before him, Charles the Bold, son and heir of Philip the Good, came into conflict with Gelderland. He had high hopes for his empire, seeking to expand it to equal the size of the former Carolingian central empire of Lothair in the ninth century. He formed an alliance with the English king, who would be willing to support him in the struggle against France, which grew uneasier as Burgundy grew more powerful. Charles the Bold annexed Gelderland to the Burgundian empire in 1473. He conquered Lorraine in the same year so that his states in the Netherlands adjoined his Burgundian lands. But in 1476 the people of Lorraine rebelled. He was killed in an attempt to regain the capital, Nancy, in 1477. He was succeeded by his only daughter, Mary of Burgundy. When she married Maximilian I of Hapsburg, Archduke of Austria, of the family which had produced German emperors for many decades, the Burgundian and Hapsburg empires were united.

Meanwhile, the Hoekse party in Holland continued to oppose Burgundy and attempted to undermine Burgundian authority. The rebels were driven to the city

of Utrecht from where, between 1481 and 1483 they carried on a bitter struggle against Bishop David of Burgundy and Emperor Maximilian of Hapsburg, the husband of Mary of Burgundy and so also the new Lord of Holland.

Mary died in 1482, and Maximilian obtained the regency for their son Philip, later known as Philip the Fair.

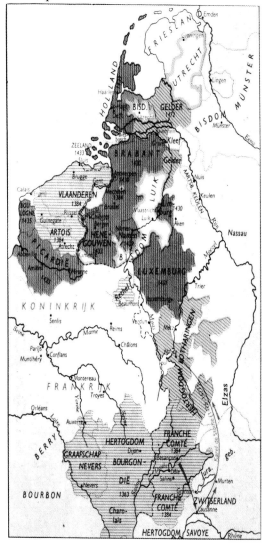

Map showing expansion of Burgundian Empire due to the conquests of Philip the Bold, Philip the Good, and Charles the Bold.

The Hoeksen were defeated at Utrecht in 1483. However, they returned to the field against the Burgundians in 1488 and even succeeded in taking the city of Rotterdam, only to be defeated again two years later. Meanwhile Gelderland was more successful in freeing itself from Burgundian bondage.

Burgundy and Hapsburg; Philip the Fair (1478-1506)

Philip the Fair, who came of age in 1493 did not at first take kindly to the idea of subjecting Gelderland once again. But on the insistence of his father Maximilian, he conquered the duchy in 1504. Charles, Duke of Gelderland then formed an alliance with the French king. He attempted to regain his lands by means of raids headed by the dreaded military commander Maarten van Rossum. He also succeeded in subduing Groningen and Friesland for a time with the help of the Frisian pirate "Grote Pier". Groningen then acknowledged him as its overlord.

The titles of Philip the Fair reveal how mighty Burgundy had become. He was Duke of Burgundy and Lord of the Netherlands regions. As his father's son he was also Archduke of Austria; in 1495 he married Joanna of Castile, the only remaining successor to her mother's kingdom of Castile and her father's kingdom of Aragon. These regions were to form the heart of Spain as it is today. On the death of his mother-in-law in 1506 Philip also became King of Castile. He died in the same year.

The tomb of Charles the Bold in the church of Our Lady, Bruges.

53

The Netherlands as part of an international union: Emperor Charles V (1500-1558)

Because of the marriage of Philip the Fair and Joanna of Castile, their eldest son Charles was destined to inherit a great empire. He was born in Ghent in 1500 and brought up in the humanist tradition by the scholar Adrian Boeyens. On the death of his father in 1506, Charles came into the entire Burgundian inheritance, including the many duchies and counties that together were now being called the Netherlands for the first time. He was declared of age in 1515, and in 1516, on the death of his grandfather

Charles V (1500-1558), Lord of the Netherlands, Emperor of the German Empire, King of Spain, etc. 'The sun never set' during his reign.

CHARLES I EMPEREVR. 34 COMTE.

Ferdinand who had governed Castile as Regent since 1506, he became king of both the Spanish kingdoms, Aragon and Castile, which also included Mexico, Peru and the Philippine islands
He also inherited the Austrian States on the death of his grandfather Maximilian in 1519; finally, by dint of much intrigue and bribery he became Emperor of the Holy Roman Empire.

All the regions of this empire remained separate administrative entities. Meanwhile, Burgundy itself had been regained by France, but Gelderland, Groningen, Friesland and The Sticht had been added to the Burgundian empire when Gelderland at last surrendered to Charles V in the Treaty of Venlo in 1543. Groningen had already acknowledged him as overlord in 1536, and in The Sticht too he had acquired secular power with the approval of his former tutor Boeyens who had been elected Pope Adrianus VI through his influence. For all his political entities in Northwestern Europe together, known as the 'Seventeen United Netherlands', Charles appointed a governor, to be stationed in Brussels. The first to be sent was his aunt Margaretha of Savoy, as he preferred to choose relatives for this position of trust; she was followed by his sister, Mary of Hungary. He himself only occasionally visited the Netherlands; Spain was his main homeland. He spent most of his time fighting his enemies: France, the protestants in Germany and the armies of Islamic Turks advancing on the Balkans and the Mediterranean.

The regions and the cities oppose the policy of centralization

The regional representative assemblies, of the Estates or 'States' composed of the clergy, the aristocracy and the towns, developed into the strongest opponents of the central authority which the Burgundians and Hapsburgers were trying to establish.

As rulers of these regions -with the title of duke, count or lord- the Burgundian Hapsburgs understood the importance of a common policy and administration for all the Netherlands, and the impossibility of maintaining the individuality of each region efficiently in this respect. They set up a well-oiled machine with a well organized civil service headed by a chancellor in every region. In addition there was an advisory body, a council of high-ranking nobles, professional administrators and lawyers. There were chambers of accounts and courts of justice in the various regions which were centralized by Charles the Bold in a General Chamber of Accounts for all his regions and a Supreme Court known as the Parliament of Mechlin.

To counteract the efforts of Burgundy and Hapsburg towards centralization, a number of towns and cities tended to take action independently. For instance, Utrecht and Amersfoort played an important part in the Hoekse and Kabeljauwse feuds between 1481 and 1483. Both cities had already withdrawn jurisdiction for capital crimes from the authority of the bishop. They elected their own town council which drew up their own statutes and even went so far as to appoint the bailiff, the local personification of princely power.

The development of central government in the regions curbed the independence of the cities during the sixteenth century, but the burghers continued to influence the administration through the clergy and the aristocrats in the regional assemblies or 'States'.

The States General and the Grand Council

The regional assemblies were also affected by centralization. At Bruges, in 1464, they convened for the first time to decide whether Duke Philip the Good should go on a crusade. They were called the "States

General" and became a permanent feature in the government of the land in the "Grand Privilege" issued by Mary of Burgundy in 1477. The Parliament of Mechlin and the General Chamber of Accounts -hated instruments of central rule- were disbanded and a Grand Council was formed with 25 members and a chancellor to assist the duchess in the administration. The regulations concerning the States General were most important; they were entitled to convene at will, and the duchess was not allowed to wage war without their permission.

Later, in 1504, the Parliament of Mechlin was reinstated as a Supreme Court, but the States General retained its powers. The Grand Council was divided into a Council of Finances, a Privy Council and the Council of State under Charles V. This last general advisory council consisted of leading civil servants and the first nobles of the Netherlands. Especially the civil servants were consulted almost daily by the Emperor's governor.

Society and economy; the growing importance of the towns of Holland

The population of Europe had fallen drastically after 1350 as a result of a series of failed harvests which led to famine and weakness. The people were an easy prey for the great plague epidemics to do their destructive work. The resulting economic depression lasted into the fifteenth century, when the first signs of recovery appeared. Grain was needed in the whole of Western Europe, and there was a rich supply of grain in the Baltic countries and in Central Europe. Precisely through its trading connections the region of Holland was now growing in importance in the Netherlands. Dordrecht was already playing a leading part in merchant trading via the great rivers in the fourteenth century because it acquired the staple right for all traffic on the

CARLVS CESAR

Von [...] [...] Granuellanus   MARIA   Vellus honum

Doctor Morus.

Als CARL den 5. gar wol betracht   Den Kunich Philips seinen Sonn   Darnach er bald das Landt verließ   L'empereur Charles le 5. cognoissant par la defaillance des forces corporelles approcher sa fin,
Daß er nam ab, an leibes macht   Erhebt er neben seinen Thron   Vnd in Hißpanien verreist   assembler les Estats du Pais-bas en la ville de Bruxelles, resinant la Seigneurie et
Beruft die Herren von dem landt   Befilt vnd gibt in seine handt   Die weltlich sorg legt er von sich   uernement desdicts Pais entre les mains du Roy Philippe son Filz et cousin: De quoy
Bey sich zu Brussel in Brabant   Daß regiment der Niderlandt   Betracht allein daß ewich reich   tost apres se partit, faisant voile en Espagne la ou il se desplestra entierement des sol
                                                                                                              L'an 1555. le 25.e d'Octob e.   des mondaines a ce de librement vacquer a la contemplation des choses Diuines:
                                                                                                                                                           metr=1-60 = fol=14 96:

16th-century engraving: On 25 October 1555, in
the presence of the States General at Brussels,
Charles V cedes dominion over the Netherlands
to his son Philip, kneeling before him. The throne
is flanked by Governess Mary of Hungary to the
right and Cardinal Granvelle to the left.

56

river Rhine in 1344. Dordrecht became a central market, or 'staple town'.

After 1400 other towns of Holland began to join in international trading, especially to the Baltic, at the expense of the old Hansa towns. Amsterdam became the most serious rival, but Hoorn and Enkhuizen also prospered during this period.

The importance of trade in the Baltic was revealed by the famine which struck the Netherlands when the passage through the Sound was closed between 1531 and 1537, as a result of a war of succession in Denmark. The time that Dutch people were able to live on the produce of their own land was long past.

Fishing also became increasingly important to the towns of Holland. The discovery, at the end of the fourteenth century, that herring could be salted, cured, and preserved in this way led to a boom in herring-fishing. The shipbuilding industry flourished once more as a result of this. Existing industries continued to grow after 1400. Leiden and Haarlem became the leading centres in the manufacture of cloth from English wool. Beer was brewed in large quantities at Delft, Gouda, Haarlem and Amersfoort, some of it for export.

Rural areas were at a disadvantage in this economic development of the towns of Holland. The towns were important to the Count of Holland - now the Duke of Burgundy and later Charles V - in view of the tax revenues. For this reason some forms of industry were forbidden in the country in order to protect their interests in the towns. Inevitably this led to urbanization, and some of the larger towns already had a fairly extensive proletariat.

Among the regions of the northern Netherlands, Holland had taken the lead in the economy and this had its effect on politics in the centuries which followed. Increasingly, Baltic trade was taken from the Hansa towns in the east of the Netherlands. As most of the towns of Holland were not members of the Hanseatic League, they did not feel bound by its regulations.

Murals in a 14th-century crypt in the church of
Our Lady, Bruges.

Culture (1350 and 1550) and new developments in religion

Renaissance and humanism

There were many important cultural developments all over Europe in the period between 1350 and 1550. The renaissance originated in Italy, where the art and culture of the period reflected a deep admiration of ancient Greece and Rome; this spirit spread slowly northwards in all but architecture, where the Gothic style prevailed for some time.

The spirit of the renaissance was linked with new ideas in the various fields of learning, termed humanism, which had its greatest champion in the Netherlands in Desiderius Erasmus of Rotterdam (1469-1536). This world-famed scholar in his own day applied the humanist principle of studying the classics in the original text, to Christianity. He published the first scholarly edition of the Greek version of the New Testament. His views on ethics and religion resembled the spirit of the Modern Devotion. He believed in tolerance and peace, advocating a sober form of religion - but within the Roman Catholic church. He expressed his ideas most fully in his 'In Praise of Folly' published in 1509.

Education and literature

Other humanists were able to propound their ideas widely because they were attached to Latin schools. These schools gradually became the leading educational institutions in the Netherlands. They were originally attached to the parish churches for the specific purpose of training the prospective clergy. As the burghers grew more affluent they too began to show an interest in education. Town councils often took it upon themselves to govern these schools. In the sixteenth century the council schools were sometimes eclipsed by private

schools. The authorities reacted by imposing fines, or by banning some subjects from the curriculum. Girls were sometimes admitted to these private schools but not to council schools. Meanwhile, in the Netherlands the provision of education for both the rich and the poor had become far greater than in most other European countries. The comparatively low percentage of illiterate people in this country never failed to astonish contemporaries in the sixteenth century.

The invention of printing in the middle of the fifteenth century started a cultural revolution, as it increased opportunities for people to buy and read books for themselves. Education and printing induced cultural development in larger groups of the population. The well-to-do burghers took up literature, which had always been strictly for the aristocracy only. Merchants, bankers and entrepreneurs formed 'chambers of rhetoric' where they studied poetry, but they also endeavoured to standardize Dutch spelling. There was a shift towards dramatic art during the sixteenth century, when both playwriting and the performance of plays became popular.

Architecture, sculpture and painting

Wealthy townspeople also began to take an active interest in architecture. They frequently built their houses of stone in the Gothic style, and they often contributed generously to the building of churches, commissioning fraternity chapels and handsome church steeples sometimes over 100 metres tall. Towns such as Amersfoort, Rhenen, Delft and Breda vied proudly with each other by means of their steeples, which often adjoined the parish church. They demonstrate how closely religion, culture

The tower of the Cunera church, Rhenen.
An example of late-Gothic architecture.

and politics were intertwined in the society of that day and age.
Before 1550 sculpture was usually inspired and commissioned by the aristocracy and the clergy. But the burghers also began to subscribe to religious art as they joined fraternities; as mentioned above, they built a chapel, or at the least they maintained an altar in the parish church. The most famous fifteenth-century sculptor was Adriaen van Wesel of Utrecht (c.1420-1500), who built an altar to the Virgin Mary in
St.James's church at 's Hertogenbosch for the Illustrious Fraternity of Our Lady.

Together with a few of its smaller neighbouring towns, Utrecht had been the cultural heart of the Netherlands since about 1400. Both the episcopacy and the often aristocratic canons of the five chapters engaged numerous skilled artists. Miniature painting blossomed here in the first half of the fifteenth century. The Book of Hours made c. 1430 for Catherine of Cleves, wife of Duke Arnold of Gelderland, is the best-known example of this art. The miniature painting of Utrecht distinguished itself from that of the South Netherlands by its realism and the choice of subjects from everyday life, characteristics which prevailed in Dutch art for centuries.
Dutch painting, which hardly existed before 1400, first appeared near Utrecht, in Gouda, Oudewater and Schoonhoven. The earliest known Dutch portrait was painted in this centre. It portrays the Lady Lijsbeth van Duvenvoirde, painted on parchment in 1430.
The flourishing cities and towns of Holland also stimulated the art of painting in the second half of the fifteenth century. The cultural centre transferred to Haarlem where several artists from Utrecht set up their easels, including Albert van Ouwater. Well-known members of the Haarlem school of artists were Geertgen tot Sint Jans (c. 1467-1495) and Dierik Bouts (c. 1475), who later moved on to Louvain.

The renaissance made rapid headway in painting and sculpture during the first half of the sixteenth century. This was mainly the result of the many journeys to Italy undertaken by artists from this time onwards. The first artist known to have made the journey was Jan Gossaert, who also worked at the court of Bishop David of Burgundy. His pupil Jan van Scorel (1495-1562), well-known for his portraits and religious works, followed his example. Lucas van Leyden (1494-1533) was famous in his own day for his portraits and altarpieces, and also especially for his engravings. This form of art was in great

demand by the wealthy burghers, partly because woodcuts were cheaper than oil paintings.

The artist Hieronymus Bosch (1450-1516) was at work in Brabant, at 's Hertogenbosch. It is sometimes said that the spirit of the middle ages was still strong in his somewhat visionary work, inspired perhaps by the misery of rural life and the persecution of witchcraft just beginning.

A new age was awakening, but the earlier ages lingered on.

Luther and Calvin

In religion, enthusiasm for the sober approach preached by the Modern Devotion at the end of the fourteenth century had completely waned. There was a growing demand for pomp and ceremony in processions, pilgrimages and church celebrations. In contrast - or perhaps to ease

An example of 15th-century miniature painting: A missal dating from c. 1464, in St. George's church, Amersfoort. The ornate first letter portrays a priest displaying the host.

16th-century wooden statue portraying St. Anna and her daughter Mary with the child Jesus.

their consciences - wealthy burghers used to bring friars from mendicant orders inside the city walls in the second half of the fifteenth century.

They felt that they were fulfilling their religious duties by giving money to these monks with their spartan way of life.

There was a religious revival in the German countries in the fifteenth century, advocating the return to a purer perception of religion and increasing opposition to malpractices which, far from being discouraged, were openly tolerated by Rome. An accumulation of church functions, the sale of positions and letters of indulgence led to the Protestant Reformation in the sixteenth century. Martin Luther, one of the first reformers, who published his ideas in 95 theses in 1517, soon found favour in the Netherlands. The central government was opposed to religious differences as they only led to political unrest. It issued the first edict against the Reformation in 1521 and ordered Jan de Bakker to be burnt at Woerden in 1525, to set an example. These reactions stemmed from the fact that a much more aggressive movement than peace-loving Lutheranism had risen in southern Germany, which appealed to the lower classes in particular. Known as Anabaptism, it spread rapidly over northwestern Europe. John Beukels of Leiden, one of the leading anabaptists in the Netherlands, also led the conquest of Münster where the anabaptists maintained a 'Kingdom of God' for almost a year. Followers of this social revolutionary movement everywhere were persecuted fiercely by the authorities after an attempt to set up a similar community in Amsterdam had failed.

Anabaptism is not to be confused with the baptist faith which was also persecuted, although it was of a more peaceable nature. This religion had many followers in Friesland where it was preached by Menno Simons.

The 'Hay-wagon' by Hieronymous Bosch (c. 1450-1516): the souls of the damned on their way to hell.

Calvinism was called after John Calvin, who preached his ideas in Geneva. His doctrine did not spread widely in the Netherlands until after 1550, when it became the foremost Protestant movement there.

Charles V was in favour of taking prompt action against Protestantism; as early as 1522 he consulted with the pope on a reorganization of the sees. However, this was seen as another intolerable example of centralized power wielded in the various regions, and it was not realized during his rule. In 1555 a Peace of Religion was signed at Augsburg , which decreed that the religion of a ruler was to be shared by his subjects. This meant that the regions of the Netherlands would be obliged to remain Roman Catholic.

Martin Luther (1483-1546), originally an Augustine monk, who protested against abuses in the Roman Catholic church. Together with other reformers he laid the foundation for Protestantism.

John Calvin, the reformer from Geneva whose dogma found a large following in the Netherlands after 1550.

▶

IOANNES, CALVINVS

Society and politics after 1550; growing opposition to 'Spanish' rule

The Pragmatic Sanction was issued by Charles V in 1549. In it he laid down a single law of inheritance for the seventeen provinces of the Netherlands, ensuring their indivisible heritage under one ruler. The provincial assemblies ratified the sanction after which Philip II, son of Charles V, made his entrance in the Netherlands as his honoured successor in all the provinces.

King Philip II (1527-1598)

Philip duly took over the government from his father in 1555. Charles retired to Spain where he died three years later. Governor-General Mary of Hungary also left her post in 1555 to be succeeded by a new governor in the years to follow. But Philip governed in person while he was in the Netherlands to wage war against France.
The administration continued as before with the Council of State as the main advisory body in name. This was headed by Antoine Perrenot, later Cardinal Granvelle, a highly influential dignitary. The Council comprised five lawyers and a number of aristocrats including the Counts Lalaing and Egmond, and William of Nassau, Prince of Orange. Like Mary of Hungary before him, Philip preferred to consult a few trusted advisors, disregarding the majority of the mighty nobles in the Council of State, who found this extremely frustrating. Among these was the Prince of Orange who owned extensive lands in Holland, Brabant, Burgundy and Luxembourg. He had been a favourite at the court of Charles V where he was befriended by Granvelle. But he fell from grace when, in 1561 against his advice, he married Anna

Philip II (1527-1598), Lord of the Netherlands, King of Spain. A portrait by Antonio Moro.

of Saxony, the wealthy daughter of one of Charles's old enemies.

Granvelle

When Philip left the Netherlands in 1559, Granvelle assumed power increasingly, to the displeasure of the governor Margaretha of Parma, the king's half-sister. It was Granvelle who excluded many members of the Council of State from its consultations, even those who had been appointed Stadhouder for the king in various provinces of the Netherlands; for instance, William of Orange who was Stadhouder in Holland, Zeeland, West-Friesland and Utrecht.

There was another way in which Granvelle was able to influence the administration. The long-awaited reorganization of the church hierarchy of the Netherlands was established in 1559. All new dioceses were placed under the supervision of the Archbishop of Mechlin, who also became the spokesman for the clergy in the States of Brabant. Formerly this had been a privilege of the abbot of the great abbey of Afflighem. In view of its high annual income, this abbey had been incorporated in the diocese, enabling the bishop to enjoy the privileges of the abbot. The new Archbishop of Mechlin was none other than Granvelle, who acquired a double hold on the government of the Netherlands in this way.

The League of the peers; the Prince of Orange and other nobles

In 1562 the dissatisfied court nobles formed a League under the leadership of William of Nassau, the Prince of Orange. They demanded that the king recall Granvelle, who had been made a cardinal in the meanwhile. They succeeded in this because the governor had her own reservations about his performance. On the pretext of a visit to relatives the cardinal left the Netherlands in 1564, never to return.

His departure gave the nobles more influence in the administration, but this was not enough to satisfy them because the land was in a state of economic depression. This was partly a result of the costly wars waged by Charles V which Philip II was still continuing. Charles had borrowed heavily at high rates of interest to finance these wars. Spain provided the Netherlands with funds from the proceeds of South -American gold and silver, but the Dutch were nevertheless convinced that their tax monies were often used in wars which were of no importance to the Netherlands. The ever higher taxation was borne under protest and the king's attempts to introduce a capital levy on trade and industry were rejected resolutely by the States General. After all, the representatives of the cities were often businessmen themselves.

The first signs of revolt

The economic situation deteriorated even further for most of the population after 1563. The Sound was closed yet again during a war between Sweden and Denmark. Merchant shipping and transports of grain from the Baltic, a lifeline of food, became impossible. When the harvest also failed, after an unusually severe winter, the people were in a mood for revolt.

Uprisings were not at all unusual in some groups of the Netherlands population. During the long period of regional independence most of the cities and regions had gained privileges which they intended to keep. If these were threatened the town would rise in revolt against the duke or count who was usually obliged to give in,

because he could not afford to antagonize his tax-paying burghers.

One of these regional privileges was the administration of justice. The people objected to a central legal body such as the Parliament of Mechlin. They objected even more strongly to the Inquisition introduced by Charles V to deal with the persecution of heretics. They were well aware that religious differences caused trouble at a local level, but they saw the persecution by the central government as interference with their own authority. It filled them with dismay to see fellow townspeople tortured or burned at the stake. The result was that no heretics were burned after 1553 in the province of Holland and the death sentence became rare in Friesland.

The difficult financial and economic situation, combined with religious persecution caused rebellious feeling to run high.

An important factor was that the Protestants had organized their movement more efficiently after 1560. Influenced by large numbers of Protestant refugees from France, the Huguenots, who had well-organized churches, many orderly Calvinist communities now sprang up in the Netherlands. Within a few years the strictly dogmatic doctrine of John Calvin had almost replaced the more moderate forms of Protestantism such as Lutheranism in this country.

The Compromise of the Nobility

Calvinism had followers among all ranks of the population. A number of the lesser nobility also sympathized with it or had

William the Silent, (1533-1584) Count of Nassau, Prince of Orange, became leader of the revolt in the Netherlands. A portrait attributed to A. Th. Key, c. 1579. (Public Information Service RVD).

▶

joined one of its churches. Like the court nobles, these lesser nobles were dissatisfied with the way the central government did its work. Moreover, their privileged position in society was endangered in both economic and military respects, by heavy taxation and armies of mercenaries. They formed their own league called the "Compromise" and presented the governor with a petition to abolish the Inquisition. This was a deed aimed at a hated *symbol*, just as it was a sign of revolt to embrace Calvinism. Signed by over 400 lesser nobles, the petition was delivered by 200 armed men on 5 April 1566. Berlaymont, a member of the Council of State, is said to have told the governor disparagingly that the men were only beggars, or 'gueux' in French. The nobles were quick to adopt the Dutch form of "geuzen".

Two court nobles, the Lords of Montigny and Bergen, travelled to Spain to present the petition to the king. Margaretha's reaction had been favourable, promising that no one would be persecuted for his beliefs, but her decision had to meet with the king's approval.
Margaretha's promise did not entirely satisfy the Calvinists who also wanted the freedom to worship openly. They held services in the open air as a form of provocation, and sometimes attended by over a thousand people. It became customary to go armed to these services and this tended to stir up rebellion.

The iconoclastic fury

Meanwhile there was a rumour that some of the leading nobles had converted to the Reformation. Egmont, Hoorne and Orange were among those suspected of heresy. They resented this bitterly and announced their intention of leaving the Netherlands, to the displeasure of the governor. She needed them to calm the inflamed Calvinists, and persuaded them to stay for the time being.

But the storm could no longer be averted, especially in the South of Flanders, that was in the grip of a deep depression. There was general unrest as a result of a shortage of food because the Sound had frozen over, and unemployment in the textile industry due to the falling supply of wool from England.
An iconoclast or image-breaking fury broke out in August 1566, causing irreparable damage in many churches; as the name implies, images and idols symbolizing the hated official church were removed, to prepare the churches for Protestant worship which did not allow images.

Pressed by circumstances, Margaretha granted the Calvinists permission to hold services openly in those areas where they were already held secretly. This satisfied the lesser nobles who promised to support the governor in maintaining order. Most of the first nobles also rallied to her side although some of them favoured military intervention.

The renewed oath of allegiance to the king

At the beginning of 1567 the members of the Order of the Golden Fleece, which included most of the leading aristocracy, as well as the government officials and soldiers were asked to swear a new oath of allegiance to King Philip II. Some of the nobles, including Orange and Hoorne refused to do so.
Hoorne later complied, but in May, when the situation deteriorated, Orange fled to Germany together with thousands of other rebels, most of them Calvinists.
Some of the most rebellious figures and those whose possessions had been confiscated took to the sea to continue the rebellion as 'Sea Beggars'.

Alva and the Council of Blood

The governor resigned her post in the same year. Her highly-coloured account of the situation led Philip to raise an army of 10,000 men which entered the Netherlands on 22 August 1567 under Don Fernando Alvarez de Toledo, Duke of Alva. Philip gave Alva almost unlimited power as the new governor-general. One of his first deeds was to set up the Council of Troubles, soon commonly known as the Council of Blood on account of the death sentences pronounced.

The king's rigorous action, prompted by exaggerated reports of the situation probably caused the Calvinistic part of the Dutch population finally to reject his authority, or rather that of his hated representatives.

William the Silent, as he became known, also suffered personal loss at Alva's hands. His eldest son Prince William, a student at Louvain, was abducted and held hostage in Spain, never to see his father again. The fellow-campaigners of Orange too, Egmond and Hoorne, were taken prisoner and executed in 1568.

Copper engraving by P. de Jode after Otto Vani, portraying Alexander Farnese, Duke of Parma (1544-1592).

'PLACCAERT

Vande Staté generael

vande ghevnieerde Nederlanden:

Y DEN WELCKEN, MIDTS
EN REDENEN IN'T LANGE IN'T SELFDE
begrepen, men verclaert den Coninck van Spaegnien vervallen vande Ouerheyt ende Heer-
schappije van dese voorf. Nederlanden,
ende verbiet fijnen naem ende ze-
ghel inde felue Landen meer
te ghebruycken, &c.

SCRVTA- MINI.

TOT LEYDEN,

By Charles Silvius / ghefworen Drurker der
Staten s'landts van Hollandt.

M. D. LXXXI.

Met privilegie voor tvveejaren.

PLACCAERT VANDE
STATEN GENERAEL VANDE
ghevnieerde Nederlanden, Bijden vvelcken, mits
den redenen in't langhe in't felfde begrepen, men
verclaert den Coninck van Spaegnien vervallen
vande Ouerheit eñ heerfchappije van defe voorf.
Nederlanden : ende verbiet fijnen naem ende ze-
gel inde felue Landen meer te gebruycken, &c.

E Staten generael vande ghevnieerde Nederlanden / Allen den ghe-
nen die defe teghenwoozdige fullen fien
ofte hoozen lefen / falupt. Alfo een pege-
lick kennelick is / dat een Pzince vande
Lande van Godt ghestelt is hooft ouer fijne onderfa-
ten/om de felue te bewaren eñ befchermen van alle on-
ghelijck / ouerlaft eñ ghewelt / ghelijck een Herder tot
bewaerniffe van fijne Schapen : Eñ dat d'onderfaten
niet en zijn van Godt ghefchapen tot behoef vanden
Pzince/om hem in alles wat hy beveelt/weder het god-
delick oft ongoddelick/ recht oft onrecht is/onderdanich
te wefen/ eñ als flauen te dienen: maer den Pzince om
d'onderfaten wille/ fonder de welcke hy egheen Pzince
en is/ om de felue met recht eñ redene te regeeren / ende
voor te ftaen eñ lief te hebben als een vader fijne kin-
deren / eñ een herder fijne fchapen / die fijn lijf eñ leuen
fett om de felue te bewaren. Eñ fo wanneer hy fulcks
niet en doet / maer in ftede van fijne onderfaten te be-
fchermen/ de felue foect te verdzucken/ t'ouerlaften/heu-
re oude vzijheit/ pzivilegien/eñ oude hercomen te bene-
men / eñ heur te gebieden ende gebzupcken als flauen/
A ij   moet

---

*Title-page and first page of the 'Act of
Abjuration' published by Charles Silvius,
Leiden, 1581.*

The struggle for independence; the 'Eighty Years' War'

1568: The beginning of the war

Meanwhile in the German countries, the Prince of Orange had raised four armies of mercenaries which were to invade various places in the Netherlands under his own leadership and that of his brothers, the Counts of Nassau. At the battle of Heiligerlee in Groningen in May 1568, the Stadhouder in Friesland for Philip II was defeated, but Adolph of Nassau was killed. Two months later this small army, now under Louis of Nassau, was defeated by Alva himself.
Prince William's own invasion of Brabant in the autumn also failed. He was compelled to retreat to Germany, disbanding the armies due to lack of funds.

When making his plans Orange had counted on support from the people. But however rebellious their mood, they were still not desperate enough to follow the Prince in overthrowing the government. This changed when, in addition to his persecution of the Calvinists, Alva introduced new tax measures. These met with opposition although they were sensible fiscal plans which would have led to a more proportional taxation. Especially merchants and entrepreneurs - the city elite - objected to Alva's plan to levy a sales tax of 10% on all transactions, known as the Tenth penny. Apart from the blow this would deal to business, it would also weaken the power of the purse of the States General and thus its leverage vis à vis the government, because these fiscal measures were to be permanent. The States bought off their obligation to pay the Tenth penny for the first two -year period, after which Alva made a fresh attempt to levy the tax in a milder form in 1571. There was resistance to this from the town councils and from the hitherto loyal members of the Council of State like Berlaymont. At this point Alva resigned, but the king asked him first to restore law and order in the land.

1572: The capture of Brill

Meanwhile, William of Orange had raised a new army with the support of French Protestants who were more than willing to combat their arch-enemy. However, his plan to attack the government troops from the south and the east failed miserably. The Sea Beggars, who were campaigning to occupy some of the important coastal towns of Holland and Zeeland, were more successful. They captured Brill on 1 April 1572, followed by Vlissingen and Veere in the same month. At last the revolt which the Prince had hoped for earlier broke out in Holland.

Most of the towns and cities rallied to his side, with a few exceptions, including Amsterdam, that feared for its commercial interests. Meanwhile, Alva was campaigning against an army commanded by Louis of Nassau in the South, so that he was unable to crush the revolt himself. An assembly of the revolutionary towns at Dordrecht elected William of Orange as Stadhouder, which meant that he still represented the king's authority. The rebels had not at first intended to withdraw their allegiance to the king, as they eventually did; they only demanded that their rights and privileges be acknowledged and that the interests of the Netherlands would no longer be subservient to Spanish policy. In a folk song written at this time -and only in the twentieth century promoted to National Anthem- William's own words were: 'I have always honoured the King of Spain'. At first the revolt seemed to spread from its starting point in Holland to the other provinces. Parts of Friesland and Gelderland were won over to the side of the Prince. But the Massacre of St. Bartholomew's Eve in Paris on 24 August 1572, during which countless Huguenots were betrayed and murdered, put an end to favourable developments. Without financial aid from France the Prince of Orange was forced to disband his army. He withdrew to Holland, the province which had been the first to support him.

1573 and 1574: The relief of Alkmaar and Leiden

Alva took revenge by sending an army to plunder some of the rebellious towns. After an unsuccessful siege of Alkmaar the Spanish troops had to retreat. Water, so often the enemy of the Dutch, came to their rescue here. The land surrounding the town was inundated by cutting the dykes, and this forced the besieging army to retreat. This event took place on 8 October 1573 and it is still celebrated in Alkmaar today as the first rebel victory.

A year later, on 3 October 1574, Leiden was taken by the rebels. In thanks to God, the first university in the northern provinces was founded here in the following year for the purpose of training Reformed preachers. The Prince of Orange had joined the Calvinist church and the tide had turned to such an extent in Holland that the States now prohibited Roman Catholic worship.

1576: The Pacification of Ghent

Don Louis de Requesens, appointed governor-general after the departure of Alva in 1573, attempted to reach an agreement with rebellious Holland at Breda, but without success. He died suddenly in 1575 after which the Spanish troops, who had not been paid for some time, advanced on Brabant and Flanders. They brutalized the population, looting and raiding the

country and threatening the towns. The Council of State now took over the government in the absence of Requesens and Spanish authority. In defiance of the king the States General were convened at Ghent where a 'Pacification' or peace treaty was signed.

In the Pacification of Ghent the Netherlands provinces were pledged to cooperate in ending the 'Spanish Fury'. However, no definite solution was found for the religious differences. The laws on persecution of heretics were suspended and Catholics outside Holland and Zeeland were to be left in peace.

The ideal which Orange had cherished over the years seemed to have been achieved; in spite of religious differences the Netherlands were united against Spanish politics and Spanish methods and there was a degree of religious tolerance.

1579: The Union of Arras and the Union of Utrecht

The rebellion also gained ground in the Southern Netherlands at first. William of Orange was even brought to Brussels in triumph. But a number of Catholic nobles resisted the rise of Calvinism and joined forces under Montigny. They sided with Philip II, forming the Union of Arras on 6 January 1579. This amounted to a declaration of allegiance to the king and to the Roman Catholic religion. The reaction to this came on 23 January 1579 in the act of Union of Utrecht, a pact between some of the northern provinces with the object of continuing the struggle against Spain together. It was signed by Holland, Zeeland, Utrecht and the Groningen Ommelanden. John of Nassau signed for Gelderland and Zutphen. In the act of Union it was agreed that the participating provinces were to remain united in a perpetual alliance, but that each was to retain its historic acquired rights. Important decisions such as declarations of war or peace and the

Der Ertz Hertzog Matthias gnant
Zu Brußell im Brabendschen land
Auch der Prins von Uranien
Jetzt ein fabel durch gans Hispanien

Gott, vnd den Staten ins gemein
Zu dem jhrm Kunig auch allein
Schweren zu bleiben hold vnd traw
Damitt das Land nun auff sein baw

On argkwon vnd suspition
Damitt sein der Hispanier hon
Entfliehen, vnd einmall sein gefreidt
Jr ordnung vnd gerechtigkheitt

Anno Dñi M. D. LXXVIII
am 20 Janua

1578: William of Orange and Archduke Matthias of Austria swear allegiance to Philip II and the States General.

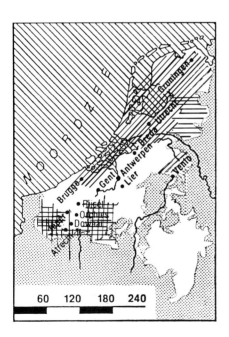

1579: the Netherlands disintegrates. A map of the Union of Utrecht and the Union of Arras. The Union of Utrecht included Holland, Zeeland, Friesland, the Groningen 'Ommelanden', Drenthe, three quarters of Gelderland, Utrecht and the 'Vrije' of Bruges. The regions which formed a pact with the Union were: Overijssel and the County of Zutphen. The Union of Arras included Artois and Hainault.

introduction of tax measures were to be agreed unanimously.

The provinces had the right to decide for themselves on religious matters, with the understanding that there was to be no further religious persecution.

1581: The Act of Abjuration: The Northern Netherlands declare their independence

The Prince of Orange, who supported the Union initiated mainly by his brother John, was formally outlawed by Philip in 1580. He advised the States General to elect a new sovereign in the person of the French Duke of Anjou. William himself would stay in power in Holland and Zeeland.

The natural sequel to this transfer of sovereignty was the Act of Abjuration of 22 July 1581 in which the States General of the northern provinces, now assembled in The Hague, withdrew its allegiance from Philip II.

The appointment of Anjou was symbolic. In fact the government was in the hands of William of Orange and the States General. The various provinces were governed by the Provincial States.

1584: The assassination of William of Orange

On 10 July 1584 William of Orange was assassinated at Delft, at the age of 51, by the religious fanatic Balthasar Gerards. The revolt had lost its leader, but this may well have taught the provinces united in the Union of Utrecht to pull together. The States General decided to entrust a Council of State with the administration of the land for the time being. Prince Maurice, the 17 year-old son of William of Orange was made a member of the Council. The son of John of Nassau was elected to become the new Stadhouder in Friesland.

The notion that a state could manage without the single authority of a personal sovereign had not yet occurred to the States.

For this reason, on the death of Anjou, sovereignty was offered first to the King of France, who refused it, and then to Queen Elizabeth of England. She promised to send someone suitable for the position of governor-general. Her choice fell on her favourite, the Earl of Leicester who was appointed in 1586. His performance during the two years of his stay in the Netherlands did not impress the new leaders. But the future looked bleaker than ever for the budding state after his departure. A huge Spanish fleet - the Invincible Armada - was on its way to the Netherlands to crush the rebellion once and for all and also to teach England a lesson. Fortunately for the rebel provinces the Armada was defeated, thanks to the bold action of Admiral Francis Drake, and later almost completely destroyed by a storm off the coast of England.

The 'Prinsenhof', Delft.
The home of William the Silent. He was assassinated here by Balthasar Gerards in 1584.

The tomb of William the Silent in the Nieuwe Kerk, Delft.

The window dedicated to William the Silent in the Nieuwe Kerk, Delft.

The 'Republic of the Seven United Provinces' on its way to independence

Prince Maurice and John van Oldenbarnevelt

It was mainly due to the efforts of two emerging key figures, Prince Maurice and John van Oldenbarnevelt, that an independent federation survived in a 'Republic of Seven United Provinces'. Van Oldenbarnevelt (1547-1619) was the senior civil servant of the Province Holland, authorized to sign resolutions on its behalf. He persuaded the States of Holland to elect Prince Maurice as Stadhouder.
Prince Maurice was a good military leader and he won many campaigns at the head of the army of the rebel provinces between 1588 and 1595, together with his cousin William Louis, Stadhouder of Friesland. The campaigns came to a halt in 1595 as the States General lacked funds to pay the troops. But in 1596 both France and England were at last prepared to support the united provinces and even to acknowledge them as an independent federation. In June of the same year Van Oldenbarnevelt succeeded in uniting the Northern Netherlands with France and England in the Triple Alliance.

The Twelve Years' Truce 1609-1621

In the year of his death, 1598, Philip II granted the Netherlands to his daughter Isabella on the occasion of her marriage to the new governor-general, her cousin Archduke Albert of Austria. In Spain the climate was ripe for a change of policy towards the situation in the Netherlands.

In the breakaway northern provinces, two trends in their attitude to Spain gradually emerged. One was for continuing efforts to win over the remainder of the seventeen Netherlands to the Revolt, the other was satisfied with the status quo.
Prince Maurice was the leader of the first group. He had his reasons for wanting to continue the war, partly out of self-interest. His one position of real power was that of Captain-General of the army. Without a war this title would lose its meaning and the Prince would lose much of his power.
Van Oldenbarnevelt led the movement for peace in which he represented the views of most of the authorities in the towns of Holland. These 'regents' usually came from leading merchant families and saw no gain in an alliance with the southern provinces, particularly Flanders with its wealthy trading towns. Trade and industry were just beginning to prosper in the north, partly as a result of their decline in the south.
Still, many of the merchants favoured continuing the war which they thought had brought them prosperity. Calvinist zealots were also for continuing the struggle against Catholic Spain, the Catholic south.
In 1609 John van Oldenbarnevelt succeeded in concluding a Twelve Years' Truce with Isabella and Albert, obviously against the wish of Prince Maurits. There were to be no hostilities during this period and the status quo was to be maintained. The archduke and his wife also agreed to acknowledge the sovereignty of the Republic on behalf of King Philip III of Spain during the truce.

Arminians and Gomarians

The opposing political views held by Prince Maurice and John van Oldenbarnevelt at the beginning of the Twelve Years' Truce were aggravated by religious differences.
Arminius had been the professor of theology at leiden since 1603. He held fairly liberal views, particularly on predestination, a cornerstone of Calvinist doctrine which holds that salvation is foreordained by God for some and not for others. It was not long before Arminius came into conflict with

Gomarus, also of Leiden, who could not see this vital issue threatened.

Both theologians soon had their own followers among the preachers and the faithful. In 1610, a year after the death of Arminius, one of his followers presented a Remonstrance against predestination to the States General, in the absence of a supreme clergical authority. This was answered by a Counter-Remonstrance from the Gomarians in 1611.

In an effort to avoid religious differences in the provinces, the States General convened the two parties for a conference, but they would not be reconciled. The conflict deepened over the following years with Van Oldenbarnevelt supporting the tolerant Remonstrants (the moderates), and Prince Maurice on the side of the Counter-Remonstrants (the strictly orthodox). The States of Holland chose the side of Van Oldenbarnevelt and the Remonstrants, relieved as they were that this group acknowledged temporal authority as supreme in religious matters as well. This did not suit the city council of Amsterdam which remained orthodox to demonstrate its political independence to the other cities and towns of Holland.

The Synod of Dort 1618-1619

Van Oldenbarnevelt believed that the provincial administration should have the last word in religious matters and it was thanks to him that the States of Holland passed the "Sharp Resolution" in 1617, rejecting a national synod to deal with the problems. They feared that the other provinces would use this religious issue as a pretext to voice their growing uneasiness over Holland's preponderance, enabling them to subject Holland to their will. Van Oldenbarnevelt also advised the town councils of Holland to employ a force of 'waardgelders' to deal with rioters. As the 'waardgelders' were to replace the regular troops led by Prince Maurice, he regarded this advice of the Land's Advocate as a direct attack on his authority as Captain-General.

As was to be expected, the majority of the provinces in the States General took the side of the Prince against Holland. In 1618 they decided to hold a national synod after all, which met at Dordrecht. The Remonstrant doctrines were denounced and Reformed orthodoxy was formulated precisely. A new translation of the Bible was also authorized at this synod. Completed in 1637 it was called the 'States Bible'; to many Protestants this was the only true Word until well into the twentieth century. The Remonstrant preachers continued their struggle in secret for the time being, but by 1630 their meetings were tolerated as before. Many of the regents preferred the tolerant Remonstrants to the more fanatical Counter-Remonstrants.

The execution of John van Oldenbarnevelt

Meanwhile Prince Maurice took high-handed action in several cities, replacing regents who sided with Van Oldenbarnevelt or the Remonstrants, by others. The States General condoned this action and gave him full power in August 1618, on which he ordered the imprisonment of Van Oldenbarnevelt and his associates.

The subsequent trial of Van Oldenbarnevelt followed by his execution in May 1619, was the culmination of political and religious differences which had developed in the young Republic. Van Oldenbarnevelt was convicted for the contents of his Sharp Resolution and for his efforts to have them observed. But in reality he was the victim of Prince Maurice's wish that the power of the Stadhouder and the States General should prevail over the independence of the individual provinces, especially that of mighty Holland which threatened to dominate the others.

Title-page of an 18th-century edition of the
States' Bible of 1637.

*The surrender of Breda to the Spanish
commander Spinola in 1625. 'Las Lanzas' by
Velasquez.*

After the death of Van Oldenbarnevelt, Prince Maurice was the foremost authority in the Republic. He also became Stadhouder of Groningen and Drenthe in 1620. At the end of the Twelve Years' Truce in 1621, he continued his successful military campaigns in the south, including the relief of the besieged town of Bergen op Zoom.

On his death in 1625, Maurice was succeeded by his half-brother Frederick Henry as Stadhouder in five of the seven provinces. Groningen elected his cousin Ernst Casimir, who was already Stadhouder in Friesland. Frederick Henry continued, like Maurice to lead many successful campaigns. He won Den Bosch, Venlo, Roermond, Maastricht, Breda, Sas van Gent and Hulst for the Republic so that part of the southern provinces of Brabant and Limburg were added to its territory. At sea, a decisive victory over the Spaniards was won in 1639, when Admiral Maarten Tromp destroyed a second Armada in English territorial waters. But an outright victory over the South by the Republic, or of the North by Spanish troops did not seem possible.

Statue of Pensionary Johan van Oldenbarnvelt (1547-1619), The Hague.

The Peace of Münster 1648: the end of the Eighty Years' War

In 1640 negotiations were started for a peace treaty between both Spain and the Republic, and between Germany, France and Sweden which had been at war for some years. In Holland, and especially in Amsterdam, people were beginning to realise that a continuation of the war would be harmful to trading interests.

But it was not until 1646 that all the provinces agreed on the necessity for peace. A delegation of the States General arrived at Münster in that year, where representatives from France, Spain and the German Emperor had already gathered. Two more years of talks were needed on matters such as the recognition of the sovereignty of the Netherlands, freedom for Dutch merchants to trade with the East and West Indies, and freedom to worship Catholicism in the Republic.

The peace treaty was finally signed in 1648. The most important clause of the treaty was the recognition by the Spanish king of the United Netherlands as a free and sovereign country. This sovereignty was also acknowledged by the German Emperor, until then still the highest power in name over the largest part of the Northern Netherlands, the eastern provinces.

Another vital clause to trade was one excluding the Spaniards from trade with areas in the East and West Indies which had been won for the Republic between 1598 and 1648. Even more important : the Scheldt was to remain closed to merchant shipping from the southern Netherlands. The position of Amsterdam as international port was assured; Antwerp was no longer able to compete. Freedom of religion was accepted, but in reality open Catholic worship was prohibited.

The Treaty of Münster marked the end of the Eighty Years' War with Spain. It was the official seal on a situation which arose in 1579 when the rebellious provinces signed the Union of Utrecht.

The political structure of the Republic

It was mainly due to the efforts of Van Oldenbarnevelt that the independent northern provinces had a well-organized administration; sovereignty lay with each of the seven provincial assemblies or States. According to the Union of Utrecht, their representatives in the States General were responsible for foreign affairs. The cities carried great weight in the assemblies. They were governed by a 'vroedschap' or city council of wise ('vroede') men who appointed civic officials and filled their own vacancies in the 'vroedschap'. This soon led to city oligarchies: a small number of regent families called the tune. In the rural areas of most provinces, power usually lay with the families of landowners who were often nobles. They were also represented in the provincial states.

The seven provinces with the right to vote in the States General were Holland, Zeeland, Utrecht, Friesland, Groningen, Overijssel and Gelderland; Drenthe also had a degree of provincial sovereignty.

There were also the 'Generality Lands' as the states of Brabant, Vlaanderen and Limburg were called, which were governed directly by the States General in which they had no representation. They had been won from the Spanish government in Brussels in campaigns from the North by the new Republic which considered them as spoils of war.
Another reason for this treatment was that

catholicism had a strong following in these areas and that there was much resentment against the enforced union with the northern provinces. In consequence, there were fears in the North that these areas would eventually betray them.

The Amsterdam Bourse, built between 1608 and 1611 by Hendrik de Keyser. Engraving by Claes Jansz Visscher in J. Blaeu.

The ratification of the 'Peace of Münster' (1648), painted by Gerard ter Borch. ▶

A Dutch-East Indiaman (Public Information Service, R.V.D. The Hague).

The economy of the Golden Age: the Republic as the centre of world trade

The economic situation in Holland and Zeeland was excellent; this was largely due to a stream of refugees form the south after the fall of Antwerp in 1585. It was not long before Amsterdam and other Northern towns had taken over the role of Antwerp, previously the foremost trading centre of Europe. Now Holland kept the Scheldt closed to shipping until well into the eighteenth century.

The other five little republics, the 'land provinces', were largely rural and their economy could not produce the same affluence which the sea provinces enjoyed. This was reflected in the tax revenues which were needed to finance the joint policy of the seven provinces: Holland alone payed 58% of the total dues.

During the first decades of the seventeenth century, the two provinces Holland and Zeeland of this small Republic grew into the centre of world trade, with Amsterdam at the hub. Several factors contributed to this; firstly, the successful development of trade in the preceding centuries; secondly, there was no central government to enforce protectionist measures. Obviously, these would not have fitted in the scheme of the seven autonomous little republics. Moreover, it was only natural that the leading merchants, who laid down the law in the administration of Holland and Zeeland, carried out a foreign policy which promoted their own trade. A third important factor was the influx of wealthy merchants from the south, especially from Antwerp.

The economic situation of the largely rural Generality Lands deteriorated because the States General did not always act in their interest. One of the prosperous cities of former times to lose its affluence because of this policy was s'Hertogenbosch, captured in 1629.

Trade to the Baltic, the Strait and England

The Netherlands had long taken part in trade with the Baltic. Amsterdam was already the European centre for the grain trade in the second half of the sixteenth century. The grain trade led to trade in all kinds of other commodities. Salt, wine and spices from southern Europe, as well as herring and textiles were shipped to the Baltic ports. The Dutch merchant fleet was so active in trade with the Baltic that almost half of the ships which passed the tolls of the Sound before 1650 were Dutch-owned. Holland and Zeeland rightly regarded trade to the Baltic as their 'mother trade'.

In addition, the 'straatvaart' or trade with southern Europe through the Strait of Gibraltar also flourished. Many of the commodities mentioned above were bought there but it was also important for export. Grain was exported mainly to Spain. Merchant shipping branched out after 1590 to find its way through the Strait of Gibraltar to the Italian ports and the Levant. Dutch traders also took part in exporting English products to the continent of Europe.

During the first century of Europe's new contacts with the outside world, the Dutch had not taken part in voyages of discovery. In the sixteenth century Spain and Portugal had become the great colonial powers. Both countries were intent on finding new trade routes and on making as much profit as possible out of the conquered areas. For instance, America was important to Spain as the source of gold and silver.
Portugal had won the monopoly in the spice

trade during the sixteenth century. When in 1580 King Philip II of Spain captured Lisbon -the main gate through which spices passed into Europe- he closed the port to the Dutch merchant fleet. Only then did the Dutch consider the possibility of fetching spices for themselves at the source: the Far East - an added advantage being that Portuguese distributors would no longer be able to push up the price. This decision was followed by Dutch expansion in America.

Voyages of discovery

The success of these ventures was mainly due to their thorough preparation. An important factor was the development of cartography, which reached an extremely high standard in the Netherlands at the end of the sixteenth century. Many enterprising and wealthy merchant backers from the Southern Netherlands also played their part, seeing to it that the expeditions were well equipped when they set out.
A wealth of information was found in a printed account of the travels of John of Linschoten, who returned to the Netherlands in 1593 after spending thirteen years in Spain, Portugal and India. This book divulged a great deal of information which the Portuguese would rather have kept to themselves.
The object of the first voyages to Asia was to discover a northeast passage, the Polar route. The most famous expedition was led by Van Heemskerck and Barends in 1596, instigated by Petrus Plancius, a minister and cartographer from Amsterdam and funded by a refugee from the South, the influential merchant Balthasar de Moucheron.
The expedition stranded at Nova Zembla where it was forced to spend the winter, but it made a great discovery in the island of Spitsbergen, later to become the centre of the Dutch whaling industry.
Between 1595 and 1599 there were two expeditions to Southeast Asia by the

traditional route around the Cape of Good Hope. The second of these, led by Jacob van Neck was a great success commercially. Subsequently, trading companies were established in several North- Netherlands ports to promote regular trade with the East Indies.

Trading posts and colonization

During the voyage under Van Neck, a number of trading posts were set up on the Moluccan Spice Islands to trade with the native population. These outposts were the earliest form of Dutch colonization. Unlike the great colonial powers of the sixteenth century, the Dutch did not take possession of lands solely for profit, or to populate them. Eventually the trading factories in the Indies slowly developed into a colonial empire which began to play an important part in the nineteenth century.

Establishment of the United East India Company or 'V.O.C.'

The trading companies launched at the end of the sixteenth century, competed so fiercely among themselves that the only way to ensure their continuing success lay in cooperation. Both Prince Maurice and John van Oldenbarnevelt worked to unite them, especially when an East India Company was established in England in 1600. Representatives from the various companies met at The Hague in January 1602 at the invitation of the States General, to establish the United East India Company. Governed by a central committee, the 'Gentlemen XVII', it was granted the monopoly in the Netherlands trade to the Indies, or Asia, for a period of twenty-one years; this was later automatically prolonged.
Though the exploits of the V.O.C. appealed strongly to the imagination, its commercial value for the Dutch economy was never more than 10% of the total accounted for in the Republic. The dividends paid were

sometimes very high, and this, together with speculation in company shares, may well have accounted for its appeal.

The Bourse in Amsterdam played an important part in transactions of this kind. It was built by Hendrick de Keyser between 1608 and 1611, in the architectural style of the Exchange in London. It was a centre of European trade in commodities and stock. From the time of its opening, weekly price lists were printed and distributed all over Europe.

Privateering and the establishment of the West India Company (W.I.C.)

In additon to Asian trade via the Indian Ocean, Dutch merchant shipping also made its way westwards at the beginning of the seventeenth century. While Henry Hudson was once more looking for a northern passage to the Indies for the V.O.C. in 1609, he discovered the bay in North America which is called after him. But the voyages across the Atlantic Ocean had a different goal to those going eastwards, namely privateering, as a weapon in the war against Spain, which continued until 1648. For this reason John van Oldenbarnevelt was not in favour of founding a West India Company at all, because it would only be a masked form of funding piracy and this conflicted with his desire for peace.

Prince Maurice did not share these scruples as it suited him to be at war; he was in favour of a W.I.C. which was established in the year of Van Oldenbarnevelt's death. Trade eventually became the main object of this company too, - particularly the slave trade from Africa to America - but as Van Oldenbarnevelt had feared, privateering took first place for a long time. The greatest prize was won by Piet Hein in 1628 when he captured the Spanish silver fleet. Piracy of this kind was actually condoned by the

View of Batavia. 17th-century. (Atlas van Stolk).

States General, as long as the victims were enemy ships.

There was also some colonization, including the Windward Islands - still part of the kingdom of the Netherlands -and Brazil. Even the metropolis now known as New York was once founded as New Amsterdam. The West India Company never fully exploited the trading potential of this settlement, perhaps because it never achieved the stature of the Dutch East India Company.

Surinam

Between 1665 and 1667 Dutch traders and settlers did their best to start a colony at the mouth of the Hudson River in the New Amsterdam area, but without success. When the English claimed this area after the second Anglo-Dutch War, the Republic was willing to accept Surinam in compensation. The W.I.C. had gone bankrupt in the meantime, but it was re-established in another form and it now acquired Surinam. The company imported numerous negro slaves from West Africa to cultivate the land and it developed into a flourishing agricultural colony with extensive sugar plantations.

The Cape Colony

In 1652 Jan van Riebeek founded a settlement on the Cape of Good Hope to serve the East-Indiamen as a staging post. The Dutch were quick to settle here followed by Huguenots exiled from France; they lived mainly by farming and cattle breeding. The native population of this black continent accepted the influx of white immigrants, but there was a fierce struggle with the negro tribes which also advanced on the area from the North during the seventeenth century.

During the nineteenth century many English and some German immigrants joined the European population in South Africa. From the very beginning, the European settlers were strongly opposed to racial mingling. The problem of segregation has become increasingly acute since the non-Western world was freed from Western domination.

The rise of industry

The flourishing of Dutch trade encouraged the rise of various industries in the seventeenth century. Shipbuilding boomed in the Zaan region and supply companies such as rope-yards and sailmakers did a roaring trade.

Trade also promoted processing industries, working with imported raw materials or semi-finished products as in sugar-refining. In addition to these trade-related industries, others also prospered as a result of growing markets and, again, especially due to the arrival of refugees from the south, many of them skilled workers. The production of cloth by the textile industry at Leiden was at its height, stimulated by the skilled Flemish weavers who introduced modern methods. Holland and Zeeland were the provinces to benefit most from the prosperity which trade and industry brought, as did Friesland, to some degree. In the other provinces agriculture was still the main source of income; there, trade and industry maintained the same low level as in previous centuries, so that the contrast with the west became steadily more marked.

The reclamation of land

The reclamation of land in the North of Holland was a direct result of the prosperity ensuing from trade and industry. Its great promoter was Dirck van Os, an executive of the V.O.C. The Beemster, a large lake, was drained between 1608 and 1610 with the technical aid of John Leeghwater and the energy provided by forty windmills. In the course of the next twenty-five years, 18,300 ha. of land was reclaimed by draining other polders in North Holland. The land was needed for cattle breeding to satisfy the demand for dairy produce at home and abroad.

The climax of this period, during which the Republic dominated European world trade, lay between 1630 and 1650. The merchant fleet at that time consisted of over 2500 ships, with at least another 2000 fishing vessels, mostly herring 'busses'. A very gradual decline began after 1650, not so much in the prosperity of the Republic as in its undisputed leading role in the world economy. England grew steadily stronger as a rival, but not before the prosperity of the western provinces had stimulated the arts and sciences to blossom in the Netherlands as never before.

The Weighing-house at Leiden, built in 1657 by Pieter Post.

Civilization in the Golden Age

The Dutch Republic as a 'burgher state'

The Republic was a polity and a society unlike most other European states in that it was steered at the highest level not by the nobility or the clergy, but by a burgher elite. The influence of the burgher culture was particularly strong in the various forms of art.

Back in the fifteenth and sixteenth centuries the burghers had first competed with the nobility and clergy in commissioning works of art, mainly collectively, and usually in the form of a building or a statue.

In the seventeenth century the part played by nobles and clergy in patronage of the arts was almost entirely taken over by the burghers, whose cultural influence was mainly noticeable in painting. Visitors to the Republic were amazed to see the number of paintings for sale at fairs and markets; even simple craftsmen and farmers possessed paintings.

Painting: genre pictures

This situation had a definite impact on the development of painting. In seventeenth-century Holland a unique style emerged , due to the many genre pictures which were painted because they appealed to the general public. The subjects were usually moralistic, in the spirit of the writer Jacob Cats, whose work was very popular partly because he advocated a judicious combination of business with pleasure that appealed to the middle classes.

Group portraits of various boards of governors of commercial companies and civic institutions were in demand as they expressed pride and status. Famous examples of this kind were painted by Bartholomew van der Helst (1613-1670) and Frans Hals (1580-1666). The best-known painting of militiamen was a 'portrait' of the Company of Captain Frans Banning Cocq which, in the romantic nineteenth century, was dubbed the most famous painting of the whole seventeenth century. Painted in 1642 by Rembrandt van Rijn (1606-1669) it is known as 'The Night Watch'.

Baroque (religious) art

In addition to the genre pictures and the landscapes, seascapes and portraits that catered for the wealthier burghers, there was also art for the aristocracy, and for the Catholics, now worshiping in private. This work was more sophisticated, relating strongly to the international baroque style of painting of the time. Artists working in this style usually came from the School of Utrecht, which was not surprising as this cathedral city remained staunchly Catholic even after the Reformation. This baroque style was accentuated when a number of artists came to Haarlem from Antwerp after it was captured. Jointly they worked towards that version of Baroque which is called Mannerism. The oldest member of this group was Karel van Mander (1548-1606), known for his 'Book of Artists' containing the biographies of some of the Dutch artists. Hendrick Goltzius (1558-1617) was a native of Haarlem, a skilled engraver who specialized in coloured wood prints.

Work of this kind, more especially depicting scenes from the Bible, was often commissioned by wealthy Catholics for their conventicles. Paintings by artists of the School of Utrecht were also in demand at the court of the Stadhouder. Frederick Henry's widow, Amalia van Solms commissioned murals for the 'Orange Room' in 'Huis ten Bosch', one of the

'The Night Watch' by Rembrandt van Rijn (1606-1669), a group portrait of the Company of Captain Frans Banning Cock, painted in 1642.

present royal palaces at The Hague. These are in truly grand style with allegories highlighting scenes from the life of her husband who had died in 1647. Rembrandt also painted for the court. He was one of the few artists outside the Utrecht School to paint religious pictures. From his earliest days as a pupil the Bible was a lifelong source of inspiration to his work.

Within this context, there is no room to treat the variety of seventeenth-century Dutch Art. One can only express wonder at the tremendous quantity of high-quality work which was produced in every imaginable genre.

Gerard Ter Borch (1617-1681) is one artist who deserves special mention here. Not because his work was more remarkable than that of his fellow-artists, but because - of his own accord - he recorded one of the most momentous events in the history of the early Republic when he depicted the ratification of the Treaty of Münster, of 1648.

Architecture: the Renaissance and 'Dutch Classicism'

During the second half of the sixteenth century the Renaissance did much to lighten Gothic architecture, mainly by the addition of decorative details . But the ideal of Italian

*The present Palace on the Dam, built in the 17th century as
the Town Hall of Amsterdam by Jacob van Campen.*

Renaissance architecture, the quest for perfect dimensions in the right proportions - embodied in the human form- had not yet been taken up in the north.

Hendrick de Keyser (1565-1621) and Lieven de Key (c. 1560-1617) were the two leading architects c. 1600, employed by Amsterdam and Haarlem respectively. Like so many artists, De Key was a refugee from the southern Netherlands.

In the seventeenth century burghers took a more active part in commissioning buildings, either collectively or privately. Wealthy Amsterdam took the lead in this respect. Drastic expansion of the city became necessary after 1600 due to the rapidly increasing population. The resulting buildings which arose along the three rings of canals between 1612 and 1672, the Herengracht, Keizersgracht and Prinsengracht gave the city its characteristic image. Many lovely houses were built along the canals, including the famous 'Trippenhuis' designed by the architect Vingboons.

These canalside houses reflected the wealth and good taste of the merchant-regents of Amsterdam. Collectively they commissioned one of the most beautiful achievements in seventeenth-century Dutch architecture; the Town Hall of Amsterdam, designed by Jacob van Campen (1595-1657). The Town Hall has some typically Dutch characteristics. The architect worked with restraint and the resulting style is sometimes called Dutch Classicism. Work was begun on the building in 1648. Still, with its sculptures and paintings telling an allegorical story depicting Amsterdam in all its glory as a world trade centre, it came to embody the ideal of the baroque, a universal work of art.

Literature: the Muider Circle

A specifically Dutch style of writing was evolving in literature. The Eglantine Chamber of Rhetoric of Amsterdam did much to stimulate this. Hendrik Spiegel (1549-1612) and Pieter Roemer Visscher (1547-1620) were among its members. Their work tended to be moralizing and this tone was later echoed in seventeenth-century painting. One of the qualities for which the Dutch were known in the following centuries was tolerance towards dissidents, and this was illustrated in the work of Dirk Coornhert (1522-1590), a follower of Erasmus.

The home of the merchant and poet Roemer Visscher, mentioned above, was the venue for a large circle of painters, writers and singers, which included his daughters Anna and Maria Tesselschade. After the death of Roemer Visscher, these gatherings took place in Muiden Castle which became a hub of cultural and scientific activity in the Republic between 1610 and 1647. The variety of religions and political backgrounds represented in the Muider Circle, reflected the tolerant social climate in the Dutch upper class during the seventeenth century. The fierce dispute between Remonstrants and Counter-Remonstrants had cast a shadow, but no lasting damage had been done.

Pieter Cornelis Hooft (1581-1647) was host to the Muider Circle. A burgomaster's son from Amsterdam, tolerant in politics and religion, he was appointed bailiff of Muiden by Prince Maurice in 1609. He wrote plays, including a comedy called 'Ware-nar', an adaptation of Aulularia by Plautus. Hooft's methods symbolized the development of literature in the Netherlands. Towards the end of the sixteenth century, writers were trying to find inspiration in themselves; seventeenth-century authors found inspiration in the classics. As a historical writer Hooft turned to Tacitus for an example.

Joost van den Vondel: the 'Prince of poets'

A regular visitor to Muiden Castle was the Catholic Joost van den Vondel (1587-1679), the greatest Dutch poet of that century and author of the tragedy *Palamedes*, written in classic style but with a contemporary plot. Vondel risked his life with this work which appeared in 1625, as its subject was the 'legal' murder of John van Oldenbarnevelt. When the Amsterdam city fathers let him off with a moderate fine, he wrote another tragedy, in defence of the Catholic Mary Stuart, Queen of Scots who was beheaded by her Protestant rival Elisabeth. A comedy by Vondel, *'Leeuwendalers'*, was performed with great success at the Amsterdam Theatre to celebrate the Peace of Münster.

17th-century engraving: Jacob Cats (1578-1660), Pensionary of Holland and one of the most popular Dutch poets of the 17th century.

Hugo de Groot: founder of international law

Another member of the Muider Circle was Hugo de Groot (1583-1645) or 'Grotius', a playwright, historian and jurist. He was the political leader of the Remonstrants, for which he was imprisoned in Loevestein Castle in 1619. He made a spectacular escape in a book chest, after which he was forced to live in exile. His 'De Jure Belli ac Pacis libri tres' - 'three books on war and peace' - which appeared in 1625, laid the foundation for international law.

Music

There was music too, in Hooft's Muider Circle. Maria Tesselschade often brought the Portuguese-Jewish singer Francisca Duarte with her. Jan Pieterszoon Sweelinck (1562-1621), organist of the Oude Kerk at Amsterdam was another welcome guest. One of the greatest organists and composers of his day, he had many German pupils. He invented the fugue which Johan Sebastian Bach later developed to perfection.

Science and education

In addition to writers, musicians and lawyers, scholars were also frequent visitors at Muiden Castle. Among these was Gerardus Voss whose name was commonly Latinized as Vossius. He was professor of history at the 'Athenaeum Illustre', a college of higher education, founded in Amsterdam in 1632 with standards on a par with those of Leiden university.

The transition to Protestantism had had far-reaching effects on education. The first university in the North was founded with the precise object of providing adequate training facilities for preachers.
There were also some changes at secondary level. Latin had been and remained one of the mainstays of education at the Latin schools, but it was now possible to take part

in religious activities without it. Services were conducted in Dutch, especially as it was essential for the propagation of Calvinism that as many people as possible could read the Bible, printed in the vernacular. As a result 'Dutch Schools' were founded everywhere, usually at the instigation of church or town councils. Only the most elementary subjects such as reading and writing were taught at these schools.

New institutions of higher education were established in the wake of the foundation of Leiden university. One such college was founded in Franeker in 1585, one in Utrecht in 1636 and another in Harderwijk in 1645. These colleges fulfilled the need for higher classical education to follow the courses which the Latin schools offered to the circles of regents and wealthy merchants in particular. Schools for middle-class children were started during the seventeenth century to provide more practical, commercial education. These were the 'French' schools where the subjects taught were French, geography and arithmetic, and also - in true Calvinist tradition - religious instruction and ethics. Most of the French schools were run privately, with boarding facilities for pupils living at a distance. They supplanted the Latin schools in many places.

All this educational activity ensured that the rate of literacy in the Dutch Republic was among the highest in the contemporary world.

The Peace Palace, The Hague, completed in 1913 as seat of the International Court of Justice. This was established at The Hague, partly to commemorate that, in the 17th century, Hugo de Groot laid the firm foundation of international law as it is today.

Society and politics in the second half of the seventeenth century

Stadhouder William II

England was the first to show hostile behaviour towards the Republic after the Peace of Münster. One reason for this was that William II supported the cause of the English Stuarts who had been banished by Oliver Cromwell after the execution of Charles I in 1649. William was married to Charles's daughter Mary.

Both for commercial and ideological reasons, most of the city regents were opposed to the Stadhouder's wish to intervene on behalf of the Stuarts. Their relationship had cooled already after the Peace of Münster had been agreed against William's will. It was not improved when, in 1650, the States of Holland announced that they would no longer support the 42 armed companies in their pay. William then caused a resolution to be passed by the States General, ordering the captains to remain in charge of their companies. He visited the cities of Holland which had the right to vote in the provincial Estates, but the opposition which met him wherever he went led him to imprison six leading regents in Loevestein Castle. Rebellious Amsterdam was even threatened by an army under William Frederick, Stadhouder of Friesland. The city finally agreed to support the Prince in the States of Holland.

The First 'Stadhouderless' period 1650-1672

William died suddenly at the end of 1650, to the relief of many. There was no immediate heir as his only son was born nine days after his death. This new situation called for a

Michiel de Ruyter (1607-1676), one of the Netherlands most renowned admirals.

'Grand Assembly' to be held at The Hague, well-represented by each of the provinces. The issues were 'Unity, the army and religion' with the provinces demanding sovereignty on each issue. To ensure their own power, they decided not to appoint a new Stadhouder for the time being.

The Navigation Act. The First Anglo-Dutch war

The continuing economic success of the Republic since the 1580's had bred jealous feeling abroad, particularly in England, where this jealousy led to a Navigation Act passed in 1651, for the protection of English shipping and trade. It ruled that European goods were only to be imported to England by English ships or by ships from the country of origin. Coastal trading with England was out of bounds to foreign shipping from then on.

This English intervention in the international free-trade system promoted by the Republic and aimed at one of the main elements in Dutch commercial succes, the freight trade, led directly to the first Anglo-Dutch war (1652-1654). It was a bad war for the Republic. After the 'Three-Day Battle' at sea the English ruled the waves, even laying a blockade before the coast of Holland.

At the negotiations for peace, representatives of the Lord Protector, Oliver Cromwell, demanded guarantees from the Republic that the House of Orange would never be reinstated in its titles. Cromwell was afraid that the Oranges would support the restoration of a Stuart monarchy. The States General and the States of Holland again held opposing views on this point and this time Holland came off best. A few weeks after the Peace of Westminster was signed in 1654, the States of Holland decided that no Prince of Orange would ever be appointed Stadhouder or Admiral of the Province again. They would also oppose the appointment of an Orange to the position of Captain-General of the union by the States General. This was known as the Act of Seclusion; it had already been secretly included in the peace treaty with England. Devised by Pensionary John de Witt of Holland, this plan met with opposition from the other provinces at first. De Witt's marriage to the daughter of a regent of Amsterdam brought this influential city into his camp, strengthening his position.

Stadhouder William III

When the Stuarts returned to the throne of England in 1660, the position of the Oranges in the Republic was reinforced, the Act of Seclusion was revoked. The States of Holland softened its anti-Orange attitude for political reasons and offered to

undertake the upbringing of young William III, now ten years old. In 1666 he became a pupil of the States of Holland, a 'ward of state', because John de Witt wanted to restrict the influence of the Stuarts on his upbringing to a minimum. By that time the Republic was again at war with England which had taken New Amsterdam from the West India Company in 1664.

This Second English war ended in a resounding success for the Dutch fleet under Admiral Michiel de Ruyter. It destroyed a large part of the English fleet during a raid on the Medway in England and even captured the flagship 'Royal Charles' as booty. This victory at sea was largely due to the efforts of John de Witt in maintaining a strong, well equipped fleet; it also made it possible to tone down the terms of the Navigation Act in the ensuing peace treaty.

Portraits of Prince William III of Orange and his wife Mary Stuart as King and Queen of England.

Pensionary John de Witt

It had happened before that a Pensionary fell victim to the ambition and drive of a Prince of Orange. The same fate lay in store for John de Witt. He had done his best to build up the fleet, but he had neglected the army. The danger of this became apparent in 1672 when French intrigue prompted England, France, and the independent principalities Münster and Cologne to declare war on the Republic - all within one month. The people and some of the regents then turned to the Prince of Orange and within two months he had been appointed Stadhouder in all the provinces, except Friesland where another member of the family already held this post. William was also proclaimed Captain-General and Admiral-General.

The Pensionary had already admitted defeat by resigning his post when the French invaded, but he and his brother Cornelis were lynched and killed by a furious mob in the Hague. The ringleaders were not punished for this shameful deed, on the contrary they were rewarded by the Prince.

The struggle for a balance of power in Europe

William III began the reorganization of his neglected army as sson as he was appointed Captain-General. De Ruyter's victories at sea forced England to come to terms with the Dutch in 1674; William's own military successes led to peace with Münster and Cologne, leaving France the sole enemy. The war which was waged until 1678 once more became a matter of personal and dynastic prestige in which, according to his critics the interests of the Republic took second place with the Prince. To William it was a war that had to be waged in order to create a balance of power in Europe, to prevent

The murder of Johan and Cornelis de Witt, 20 August 1672.
Engraving by Romeyn de Hooghe, 1672.

France from achieving supreme power, and thus to secure continued independence for the Dutch. This modern concept was to become a determining feature of many later wars.

As in 1648, the regents could see no point in prolonging a costly land war that damaged their commercial interests in France; they urged the Prince to come to terms with France. The Treaty of Nijmegen was negotiated in 1678 to the fury and disappointment of the Prince.

However, William III eventually succeeded in reconciling the Republic to his struggle for a balance of power. His marriage to Mary Stuart, the daughter of James II of England, enabled him to become King of England in 1689 after his father-in-law had left the country in a state of political and religious turmoil. He then achieved his greatest wish of a Grand Alliance against France in which England, the Republic, the German Emperor, Spain and some of the German principalities were united.
Louis XIV took the side of James II in his attempt to regain the throne, but his main aim was to conquer the Spanish Netherlands and the Republic. This marked the outbreak of a Nine Years' War between France and the anti-French coalition.

Meanwhile William had decided that the Dutch should provide most of the resources for the war on land, while the English were to take the lead at sea. In so doing he unwittingly created a situation in which the maritime supremacy of the English both in war and in peace grew ever stronger; the Republic lost its leading position in world trade.
For a long time France was the strongest in combat on land, but at sea she was no match for the combined English and Dutch fleets. The war dragged on without a final victory for either side until, in 1697, the French interest in the War of the Spanish Succession took precedence over their wish to possess the Southern Netherlands. The Peace of Rijswijk was signed in 1697 which allowed the Republic to garrison a number of fortressed towns in the Southern Netherlands, as a barrier against the old French enemy.

*The 'Admiraliteitshof' at Rotterdam, seat of the
Admiralty on the Maze. Copper engraving by
J. de Vou, 1694.*

Family group portrayed in 18th-century interior,
by H. Pothoven (Historisch Museum,
Amsterdam).

Society, politics and the economy in the late seventeenth and the eighteenth centuries

The seventeenth and eighteenth centuries are always described as two contrasting periods in Dutch history, but many eighteenth-century developments originated in the second half of the seventeenth century. There is certainly no question of a sudden decline of the Dutch Republic on all fronts, as is often put forward. It was more of a gradual change in the economic and social climate, from vigorous and progressive to static and conservative. The need to make itself felt in the arena of European politics was satisfied once the Republic had found its niche among the other states. Conservatism now prevailed. The Republic continued to play a part in world trade and there was no noticeable overall decline. But the competition from other countries, including England and France, prevented the country from holding any further monopoly position. Thus it slowly lost its pre-eminence.

The decline of industry

The money market prospered during the period. In the early part of the seventeenth century many wealthy merchants had invested in Dutch imaginative and even grandiose projects involving trade, industry and agriculture. The reclamation of land in North Holland for dairy farming was financed mainly by capital gains from trade profits. In this way one enterprise led to the next. But in the eighteenth century investments were more often made abroad, especially in England.

Dutch international trade did not decline noticeably until fairly late in the eighteenth-century, but industry began to dwindle earlier. Partly as a result of the high wages paid here, production in the textile industry at Leiden dropped by 80% between 1670

and 1795. Shipbuilding too, which had flourished in the Golden Age was now in recession.

Declining investment in domestic enterprises and the relatively high wages customary in the Republic, resulted in a high level of structural unemployment and poverty in the population. As the small group of wealthy investors grew wealthier, the social contrasts were greater than ever before.

The regents and the administration until 1747

Another cause of the widening gap between social groups was the concentraton of power in the hands of a few leading families, both in the towns and in the country. There had been city oligarchies in the seventeenth century, but it had still been possible for new families to join the circle of regents, as others disappeared. In the eighteenth century this became almost impossible; in almost all the cities most of the positions, from the highest to the most humble were actually held by a few regent families. They drew up mutual agreements, so-called 'contracts of correspondence', promising not to appoint anyone from outside their circle to any post. Agreements of this kind led to the appointment of newly-born babies to offices which were carried out by substitutes for a fraction of the actual salary. This form of nepotism and patronage bred corruption and dissatisfaction among the patricians who did not belong to the regent circle.

The increasing conservatism of the regents also influenced foreign policy. Grand Pensionary Anthony Heinsius of Holland carried on the policy of William III to curb the power of France, during the War of the Spanish Succession. But once the Treaty of

Utrecht had been signed in 1713, there was no further incentive to take part in foreign affairs. In this way the Republic lost prestige and failed to take a significant part in international affairs during the eighteenth century.

Part of the reason for this indifference to foreign affairs was the fact that the treasury was almost exhausted when the Treaty of Utrecht was signed. To improve matters, Adolf Hendrik, Count of Rechteren, called for a Grand Assembly to be held at The Hague in 1716, for the second time in the history of the Republic. At this meeting the secretary to the Council of State, Simon van Slingelandt, proposed radical governmental reforms. The existing system of decision making, by which provincial delegates had to consult their colleagues at home on every proposal put forward in the States General, led to endless delays. But the delegates at the Grand Assembly were subject to the same consultations, so no agreement was reached and everything continued as before.

The Second Stadhouderless period (1702-1747)

When William III died in 1702, it looked for a while as though the House of Orange had no further part to play. He was the last direct male descendant of William the Silent. The title of Prince of Orange passed to the Frisian line of the Nassau family. But John William Friso, Stadhouder of Friesland and Groningen, was drowned in 1711. His widow Maria Louise van Hessen-Kassel governed for their son William Charles Henry Friso, who was born posthumously. She won widespread respect so that, when William came of age, he was able to take his place as Stadhouder in these two provinces without opposition. Gelderland also accepted him as Stadhouder. The remaining provinces, led by Holland, chose to continue this second Stadhouderless period of government. William's marriage in 1734 to Anne, daughter of the new Hanoverian

King of England, illustrates the importance still accorded to the title and status of Stadhouder abroad.

It was not until 1747, when the Republic became involved in the war of the Austrian Succession and invasion by French troops was imminent that, just as in 1672, the then Prince of Orange, William IV, was invited to become Stadhouder in Holland, Zeeland, Utrecht and Overijssel. The Republic was involved in this war as a result of the Treaty of Vienna signed in 1731. This treaty between Austria, England, Spain and the Republic had important political and economic aspects. The countries involved acknowledged the right of Maria Theresia, daughter of the Austrian Emperor, to the succession in the lands under his rule. Since the Treaty of Utrecht of 1713 these included the Southern Netherlands. The Republic asked a price for its involvement in the Treaty of Vienna; under the treaty the Ostend Company, established in the Southern Netherlands in 1722, was dissolved as it had become a threat to the Dutch East India Company.

When Maria Theresia claimed her rights on the death of her father in 1746, other pretenders appeared on the scene. In the European war which followed the Republic was bound by the treaty to furnish troops, but it waited so long before doing so that it lost respect. Moreover, the King of France declared war on the Republic, England and Austria in 1744 and French troops invaded the Southern Netherlands, capturing some of the fortressed barrier towns. By 1746 the south was almost entirely in the hands of the French; Flanders was occupied in 1747.

The House of Orange: William IV and William V hereditary Stadhouders in all provinces

The threat of war in 1747 and the mounting dissatisfaction with the rule of an ever more closed regent oligarchy led to spontaneous and popular movements in many of the towns, asking for the recognition of William IV as hereditary Stadhouder in all provinces. Encouraged, wealthy non-regent burghers took the opportunity of seizing power by joining the cause of the House of Orange. They were Orangist for political reasons, and as they regarded themselves as loyal to the 'fatherland', they became known as 'Patriots'.

In the following year the Treaty of Aix-la-Chapelle- marked the end of the war. The Prince, safely installed in all provinces, was now free to deal with the many forms of corruption in the administration of the Republic. He was authorized to appoint regents at the local, regional and national level. But instead of doing away with the

abuses of the former period, the Prince took the opportunity of appointing his devotees everywhere. This was a bitter disappointment to many of his supporters. There was serious rioting in Amsterdam in 1748 when the 'Doelisten' voiced their demands after a meeting in the Doelen Gallery. These demands included openness in appointments to offices, restoration of the privileges of the guilds and the allocation of the high proceeds from the postal service to the state. William IV came to Amsterdam in person and agreed to the demands.

But it was not long before things went on as before which led to a growing tendency among the educated non-regent burghers to unite in groups which voiced ever more democratic ideas. A new party emerged from this, formed by the old regent aristocracy which fell from grace in 1747, and the wealthy, non-regent burghers who still had no say in politics. They had

18th-century view of Palace Het Loo at Apeldoorn, a water-colour painting by Jan de Beijer. The carriage of Prince William IV is seen approaching the forecourt.

18th-century painting by T.P.C. Haag portraying Prince William V - in scarlet coat with golden star - welcoming the Civic Guard in the gardens of Het Loo.

different aims, but they shared their dissatisfaction with the Stadhouder's administration which was stronger than ever before. This party also called itself Patriotic, but it differed from its fellow-Patriots of 1747 in that it was anti-Orangist. Its main aim was constitutional reform of the decayed administrative system.

On the death of William IV in 1751, his widow governed during the minority of their son William V, with the Duke of Brunswick acting as Captain-General. He was an Austrian field marshal, who had been employed the previous year to build up the Republican army and he had gained great influence with the Orange family.

In the following years there was a bitter struggle between Amsterdam and William V, now of age, to decide whether to equip the army or the fleet. As usual the Prince of Orange favoured the army which would strengthen his own position, while naval Amsterdam was for the fleet. It was only in 1777, when England went to war against her American colonies, that the Republic finally decided to equip twenty men-of-war.

The support then given to the American rebels by the more democratic Dutch did not improve relations between this country and England. The decision of the States General to provide convoys for the protection of the merchant fleet made matters worse. In December 1780 the Fourth Anglo-Dutch War broke out during which Dutch maritime trade was very seriously damaged by the superior English navy.

Patriots and Orangists

The political differences between Patriots and Orangists now emerged clearly, as the Patriots blamed the Prince for this disaster because he had always opposed enlarging the fleet.

An anonymous pamphlet was distributed in 1781 describing Patriot ideology. It was headed 'To the people of the Netherlands' and written by John Derk van der Capellen tot den Poll, a nobleman of Overijssel. He asked for reform but also advocated volunteer corps of armed civic guards which were duly mustered everywhere in the following years.

During this period party politics developed gradually, not only on a theoretical basis, but also, very importantly, in practice, for the first time rising above the provincial level. Patriots from all over the country now met to draw up a kind of party manifesto. Patriotic newspapers such as the 'Lower-Rhine Post' were instrumental in this. In 1784 this paper exposed the existence of the 'Consultation Act', an agreement between the Duke of Brunswick and William V, signed in 1766 when he had just come of age. In it the Prince assured the Duke that he was only answerable to himself for any advice he might give him in the future. When this was publicized the indignation it caused was exaggerated, but the duke had to leave the country and the anti-Orange mood deepened.

The Patriot movement found further inspiration in the successful American struggle for independence. At a congress of volunteer corps it was decided that the Republic should also be governed by representation. Some of the Patriots drafted a new constitution closely resembling the American Declaration of Independence.

The Province of Utrecht had always been a Catholic stronghold with a capital city where the traditions of the guilds were still respected. Now it became the centre of the Patriot movement. However, when a democratic administration was formed in this province in 1786, the rift in the movement due to the different backgrounds of the Patriots became apparent. The dismissed regents of 1747 were only in favour of abolishing the system of patronage in appointments as applied by the House of Orange since then. But they could not agree to the far-reaching plans for reform drawn up by the burgher-Patriots. With anti-Orange feeling still deepening and the States of Holland, Zeeland, Groningen and Overijssel even suspending the Prince as Captain-General in 1786, he still remained popular with the general public. But, due to some unpolitical moves, in 1787 he felt forced to call on his brother-in-law, the King of Prussia, to intervene on his behalf and reinstate him in his former position of power. This act of force was succesful. The States of Holland were compelled to reverse all anti-Orange measures. But many Patriots fled to France, from where they continued the struggle with renewed vigour. William's move was deeply resented in the Republic.

*Palace Het Loo at Apeldoorn after its restoration
in 1984, with gardens and fountain.*

Culture in the late seventeenth century and in the eighteenth century

Flourishing activity is followed by consolidation

Life in the Republic during the first half of the seventeenth century had been marked by flourishing activities of all kinds. The second half was quieter, as though it had lost some of its sparkle. Cultural activities began to take place in a rural setting as many wealthy merchants bought country houses, some with manorial rights. Life in the country was idealized, and this is noticeable in the literary work of the second half of the seventeenth century.

Idyllic landscapes were already popular in the 1840s; Jan Both (1618-1652) and Nicholaes Berchem (1620-1683) painted works of this genre.

There was a general trend in favour of French culture among the upper classes. It was fashionable to speak French and they adopted French tastes in clothing and interior decoration. Of course this was due to the glittering court of King Louis XIV at Versailles. This court became the cultural centre of Europe in the second half of the seventeenth century, and around c. 1700 its splendour came to influence culture in all the surrounding countries.

Architecture and interior decoration

At the end of the seventeenth century the influence of French taste and culture became stronger in the various forms of art. The arrival of numerous Huguenots also brought French styles of architecture, interior decoration and furnishings. The artist Daniel Marot (1663-1752) was one of the newcomers; an engraver and interior decorator, he later worked as an architect. One of Marot's architectural designs was the Hotel Huguetan at The Hague. Marot also designed the interior of the palace Het Loo at Apeldoorn while he was employed at the court of Willem III. The delicate baroque style of this building was repeated by various other architects later in the eighteenth century.

Comprehensive designs for decorations and furnishings for whole interiors were new to the Republic and Marot and his followers created the trend. They also influenced the popular form of interior decoration practised in many parts of the country until well into the twentieth century. The beautifully painted interiors and the furnishings of houses at Hindeloopen in Friesland and the Zaan in North Holland, were imitations of the styles popular at court and in stately homes at the beginning of the eighteenth century.

Later on in this century, new styles of architecture and decoration were adopted. The architect Leendert Viervant designed a country house known as the Pavilion for the banker Hope in Haarlem, in neoclassical style.

Painting

Painting suffered most from the widening gap between the different social groups. At the beginning of the seventeenth century art, at least partly, still reflected the life of ordinary people, which served as a colourful source of inspiration for genre painting. But this kind of work was not in demand with the people who bought or commissioned paintings in the eighteenth century. Bourgeois complacency looks out at us from the eighteenth century paintings by Wijbrand Hendriks (1744-1831), Adrian de Lelie (1755-1820) and John Ekels (1759-1793), the only high-light being the work of Cornelis Troost (1697-1750). Painting was also influenced by French taste in interiors; walls were covered with decorative murals and painted wallpaper so that there was

The bedroom of Princess Mary, wife of Prince William III, in Het Loo. Decorations on the walls and the bed were restored to designs by Daniel Marot.

Example of Hindeloopen interior decoration: folk art based on 18th-century aristocratic interior designs.

little space for paintings. As a result, the art of painting wallpaper flourished in the second half of the eighteenth century. It was fashionable to depict arcadian scenes of refined pastoral life; unfortunately most of this work has disappeared over the years as fashions changed.

Literature

Wealthy burghers also followed fashion in promoting literature. An example is the foundation of the Society for Dutch Literature at Leiden in 1766. The members held monthly meetings, published their own works and maintained their own library. At first, French taste also prevailed in literature and the resulting work was not outstanding. But the tentative beginnings of an individual style appeared during the last decades of the eighteenth century. The facts about Dutch middle-class society were revealed in light satyrical vein; the best work of this kind was written by the ladies Wolff (1738-1804) and Deken (1741-1804). Betje Wolff lived with her friend Aagje Deken in De Rijp after the death of her husband. They wrote several novels together in the form of correspondence, following the example of the English author Samuel Richardson. The best- known of these novels is 'Sara Burgerhart' which appeared in 1782.
Another author looking for renewal at the end of the eighteenth century was the Pensionary of Leiden, Hieronymus van Alphen (1746-1803). Well-known to the general public for his children's verses, he was however a versatile writer and influential cultural journalist who also published an introduction to new aesthetics.

Science and religion

In addition to the interest which they took in the fine arts, educated Dutch burghers also stimulated the exact sciences. These wide interests were in keeping with the rationalistic outlook on life which had been growing since the seventeenth century. Natural science was the particular centre of attention. The Dutch Society for Science was founded at Haarlem in 1752 to stimulate scientific research. It held competitions asking for essays on physical subjects, often setting specific problems which, if solved, could lead to industrial application or other practical results. Similar societies were formed in other places and knowledge was amassed to the benefit of all by the members who stemmed from regent and well-to-do burgher circles alike, who read scientific books (together) and experimented in physics.

Rationalistic thinking was also applied to religious matters. The French Encyclopedists believed that the world was created by a God, but that it had afterwards developed along independent lines; there was a great deal of support for this view in Dutch educated circles, leading to all kinds of religious speculation and, though not widely, to a new spirit of free thinking.

The Hague: originally 'Huis Huguetan', designed by Daniel Marot c. 1734; at present the seat of the Supreme Court of the Netherlands.

Rutger Jan Schimmelpenninck, 1805-1806
Pensionary of the Batavian Republic.

Society and politics (1787-1815); revolt and foreign rule

By the end of the eighteenth century, inflexibility and conservatism had penetrated so many aspects of life in the Republic that they were bound to awaken the fighting spirit eventually. The gap between the well-to-do burghers and the lower classes mentioned above was one of the main problems. The dissatisfaction of many educated people with the ruling elite was another. Also the revolutionary spirit based on rationalistic ideas which appeared in North America and France at the end of the eighteenth century was alive in the Republic. But the dissatisfied elements lacked the solidarity to bring about a revolution. The mob which was instrumental in bringing the revolution in France to its first successes, was mainly Orangist in the Republic.

The Batavian Republic 1795-1806

In 1787, the revolt against the power of the Stadhouder had been crushed for the time being. In the following year, all the regents had to swear allegiance to the existing constitution and the provinces agreed mutually to safeguard the position of Stadhouder.
When as a consequence of revolutionary developments in France, French troops invaded and occupied a large part of the Republic in 1795, this was partly at the instigation of the Patriots who had fled to France in 1787. Those in favour of reform now took the opportunity of seizing power, headed by Rutger Jan Schimmelpenninck (1761-1825). The Batavian Republic was proclaimed and Stadhouder William V fled to England.
Constitutional reforms were soon carried out, some of them modelled on the French system. Elections were held for a National Assembly to replace the States General. All male members of the population over the age of 20 and of fixed abode were eligible to vote if they were not living on charity. Another condition was that they had to forswear the Stadhouderate.
The first meeting of the National Assembly was held on 1 March 1796 and a committee was formed to draft a constitution. But the Assembly was divided by a controversy between federalists, who were in favour of maintaining provincial independence, and Unitarians, who were against it. After much bickering a constitution based on unitarian principles was adopted in April 1798 which divided the country into eight departments. Local and departmental authorities were to be elected by those eligible to vote. The same applied to the Legislative Assembly, a national body with the power to appoint the Executive Council of five executives. This constitution became effective during the same year.
Centralization of government was realized gradually by various measures and this contributed to a growing national unity.

But in 1801 a coup was staged by the French commander, General Augereau with the help of three members of the Executive Council, to bring the Republic into line in support of France in its anti-English policy. A new constitution was implemented on some points returning to the situation as it was before 1795.
In 1805 there were consultations between Napoleon and Rutger Jan Schimmelpenninck, the Netherlands' envoy in Paris. Napoleon favoured the introduction of monocratic rule because he expected that the Netherlands' support in the struggle against England would then be well-organized. Schimmelpenninck later presented the voters with a draft constitution granting executive power to the Pensionary.

*Scheveningen 1795: the departure of
Prince William V.*

He himself would be the first to hold this office. There was also to be a Legislative Assembly of 19 members authorized to appoint the Pensionary and with the right to vote bills.

Schimmelpenninck had several able ministers at his disposal and with them he pursued a progressive policy. National regulations for elementary education were provided in the Education Act of 1806. The responsibility for education now fell to the state instead of to town councils, the church or private schools. A teacher-training school was also founded to guarantee a certain standard of education.

Unfortunately Schimmelpenninck had to resign his office after only a year when, in 1806, Napoleon proclaimed the Batavian Republic a kingdom, with his youngest brother Louis Napoleon as its unwilling king.

Meanwhile, the economy of the Netherlands had declined steadily since 1795. Overseas trading came to a standstill. The Dutch East India Company suffered such heavy losses

Louis Napoleon Bonaparte (1778-1846),
King of Holland from 1806 until 1810.

in the last quarter of the eighteenth century that it was threatened with liquidation. The Batavian Republic took over its debts and assets in 1798, and on 31 December 1799 this renowned and once so successful trading company ceased to exist. The West India Company had already been disbanded in 1791.

Industry, too, was in a poor state. Small-scale business accounted for most of the production. There was no question as yet of technical innovations such as those introduced in the Flemish textile industry. Private enterprise by wealthy burghers was not to be expected, especially as they had made a loss on their investments when the national debt was reduced by a third as a result of the annexation by France.

As the country was ever more closely allied to France during this period, it became involved in several wars with England, which occupied the Dutch colonies, one by one. Most of these overseas territories were eventually returned at the London Convention in 1814.

In 1798 there was a breakthrough in religion when Church and State were formally separated. All religious denominations were now equal in the eyes of the law: the Roman Catholics and the Jews, the largest religious minorities, were permitted to practise their religions once more.

The Kingdom of Holland under Louis Napoleon 1806-1810

Though the new king had accepted his throne under protest, his government certainly was not unbeneficial. On a number of counts, it pursued the centralizing, rationalizing policy set out in the preceding years.

A civil code was introduced on French lines in 1809, and in 1810 the Registry Office was opened for the compulsory registration of births, deaths and marriages; many families were given a name for the first time.

Louis Napoleon encouraged a number of important cultural developments. The Royal Institute for Science, Literature and the Arts was founded at his instigation in 1808. One of the tasks of this institute was to organize an exhibition of work by contemporary Dutch artists, to be held every other year. Louis Napoleon also paved the way for the 'Rijksmuseum'of later date. He started a Royal Museum in part of the old Town Hall of Amsterdam which he used as a Royal Palace. Most of the works which he kept

there came from the former Stadhouder's collection, but he took pleasure in adding to it. For instance, he included Rembrandt's Night Watch which still belonged to the city of Amsterdam, although it was not at all popular at the time.

Louis Napoleon's reign was cut short by the unsuccessful English invasion of Zeeland in 1809. He even attempted to defend the country entrusted to him against an army sent by his brother, the emperor, but the Dutch did not dare to support him. He abdicated in favour of his small son in 1810.

The Netherlands annexed by France

By this time Emperor Napoleon had already decided to annexe the Netherlands to France, to realise an old ambition viz the possession of the Rhine Delta.

Conscription to military service, determined by lot, was introduced in 1811 to bring Napoleon's army up to strength. As a result, nearly 15,000 Dutch soldiers were forced to accompany Napoleon on his ill-fated Russian campaign in the following year. Very few of them survived this terrible experience. This, and the economic recession which set in when the Netherlands was forbidden to trade with England or non-European countries, caused anti-French feeling to run high. As always in a crisis, the people turned to the House of Orange. The defeat of Napoleon by a European coalition at Leipzig in 1813, signalled the retreat of French troops from Dutch soil. The Orangist regents Van Hogendorp, Van der Duyn van Maasdam and Van Limburg Stirum took power and governed the land awaiting the return of the Oranges.

'Huis ten Bosch', summer residence in the
Hague Woods built in mid-17th-century for
Stadhouder Frederik Hendrik by the architect
Pieter Post. Daniel Marot added two wings and
a porch to the palace in the 18th-century. King
Louis Napoleon made use of it briefly in 1806.
At present it is the home of Queen Beatrix and
her family.

King William I at Het Loo with his family.
A painting by L.J. Goudband, 1830.

Society, politics, economy and culture in the Kingdom of the United Netherlands 1815-1839

Reunion of the Northern and Southern Netherlands: the constitution of 1815

At the invitation of the three interim governors, the heir to the House of Orange landed at Scheveningen on 30 November 1813. He was the son of the last Stadhouder William V, who had died in exile. The prince was inaugurated as the sovereign ruler, King William I (1772-1843) at Amsterdam on 2 December. In 1814 he also accepted sovereignty over the Southern Netherlands.

He proclaimed himself 'King of the Netherlands' in 1815, thus reuniting the seventeen provinces of the Northern and Southern Netherlands after a separation of over 225 years.

But the differences in economics, religion, culture and politics had grown so great that this union could not survive for long. One of the points of friction was the composition of the Lower House. The population was greater in the South than in the North, but 55 members from each part were represented in the House, with meetings held alternately at The Hague and Brussels. Soon the Southern members, representing a mainly Roman Catholic population complained of strong discrimination against them and began to sabotage many government proposals. The King was obliged to rule by Royal Decree which itself raised more opposition, now also from liberals in both North and South. There was even an 'unholy alliance' between Southern Catholics and the liberals in 1828.

Denominational education was one of the main problems as it required permission from the state authorities for its provision. Education in the South had always been the province of the Roman Catholic Church so that this measure was felt to be intolerably patronizing.

Language was another problem. William I decreed that the civil service was to use Dutch, in an effort to unite the two areas in one national culture. But in Flanders the upper classes usually spoke French.

Censorship of the press also caused trouble. People were taken to court for insulting the government or even for voicing critical remarks about government policy; this added to the strain on the relations between

Portrait of King William I by J.B. van de Hulst.

William I and his Southern subjects. When an industrial crisis threatened in 1830, with the Southerners blaming a free trade policy in which their industrial products were not protected in any way while Northern commerce was unduly favoured, all the ingredients of rebellion were present.

The establishment of the Belgian State: 1 October 1830

After some rioting and disturbances in Brussels and other places in the South, a temporary administration was set up by dissatisfied Southerners in September 1830. An independent state called Belgium was proclaimed on 1 October and a national conference was convened.

In November the foreign powers interested in the status of the Netherlands, including Russia, England France, Prussia and Austria met in London. A month later the Kingdom of the Netherlands had been dissolved and in January 1831 the separation of Belgium was dealt with in a number of clauses.

The King was prepared to accept the decisions of the conference, but the Belgians felt slighted by some of the clauses. A later proposal made in June was acceptable to the Belgians, but not to the King. Meanwhile, Leopold of Saxe-Coburg was elected King of the Belgians.

William I persisted in refusing the new proposals. In August the notorious Ten-day Campaign took place, during which the Dutch army initially defeated the Belgians, but was forced to retreat when the French intervened.

Hostilities were suspended in 1833, but it was not until 1838 that William I agreed to the clauses drawn up at the London Conference. The final treaty, acceptable to all parties was signed in 1839; it marked the end of the brief reunion of the Southern and Northern Netherlands. Since then the North has been known as the Kingdom of the Netherlands.

William I, the Merchant-King: trade and industry

During his reign William I met with increasing resistance from parts of the population because of his high-handed behaviour, but his contribution to economic revival in both North and South was tremendous. He earned his nickname of 'merchant-king' by his tireless efforts to restore prosperity to the Netherlands trade and industry. One of his measures was to set up the Dutch Trading Company. The King personally invested 4 million guilders in this company and guaranteed the other shareholders a dividend of 4% for the first 25 years. After 1830 the activities of this company were concentrated on trade with the Netherlands East Indies. Governor general John van den Bosch introduced the system of enforced farming. Native farmers were forced to cultivate a fifth of their land with crops ordered by the government. The resulting products such as coffee and sugar were shipped to the Netherlands by the Dutch Trading Company. Return cargo consisted of cotton clothing from Twente, among other things. In this way the Netherlands industry was supplied with raw materials and trade found an outlet. The cotton industry was set up in Twente in 1833 for the manufacture of goods mainly for the Indian market. Its succes was partly due to the dwindling Belgian textile industry.

There were other ways in which William I tried to stimulate the economy. The Bank of the Netherlands and the Mint were established on his instigation to ensure control of the money market. He also improved transportation by promoting road-building and repairs, and the construction of canals. The North Holland Canal connecting the capital with the open sea, re-opened the port of Amsterdam to large vessels. At the end of William's reign in 1839 the first of the Netherlands railways was opened between Amsterdam and Haarlem.

Private enterprise was also instrumental in making the Netherlands a great trading power once more. The Steamship Companies of Rotterdam and Amsterdam were founded in 1823 and 1825 respectively, and together they built up the modern shipbuilding industry.

Though the economy was gradually recovering, there was widespread poverty in the first decades of the nineteenth century. The so-called 'Relief Company' was founded in 1818 to combat this by providing employment for those who had not been able to earn a living before. The development of waste land was undertaken in Drenthe, in preparation for agriculture and cattle breeding.

The reclamation of one of the last remaining lakes, called the Haarlemmermeer, also created a large stretch of new land. Plans were even made for the reclamation of the Zuiderzee at this time. Of course these measures could not eradicate the basic problem of poverty.

Many of those dependent on the land decided to leave home and seek their fortunes abroad. In the course of the nineteenth century the United States of America, with its promise of unlimited possibilities became their new fatherland , but many emigrants continued to cling to their own culture for generations.

Culture and religion under William I

William's policy in promoting the Dutch language for the good of a common culture was also reflected in national symbols used in painting. Historical painting flourished and subjects from the history of the Netherlands in the sixteenth and seventeenth centuries were firm favourites. In the nineteenth century this earlier period took on its image of a 'Golden Age' on

which the Dutch looked back with justifiable pride.

In the same spirit, William I wanted to make the Reformed Church a haven for everyone in the Netherlands. This was unacceptable to some dogmatic movements, resulting in a schism in 1834. The government reacted so harshly against this that many of the followers of this puritan group decided to emigrate to the U.S.A.

Though the law guaranteed freedom of religion, there was no real equality in this field as yet.

The abdication of King William I: 1840

After a controversial reign lasting 27 years, William I had alienated himself from the people by his high-handedness, but he had worked wonders for the economy, promoting and developing prosperity in the land. However, he was compelled to abdicate in favour of his son in 1840. His position had become intolerable when, after the death of his first wife, Frederica of Prussia, he announced his intention of marrying a Roman Catholic, the Belgian Countess Henrietta d'Oultremont. After his abdication he left for Berlin where he died in 1843.

Colour litho showing the Rijnspoorweg station at Utrecht, already one of the busiest railway junctions in the Netherlands during the second half of the 19th-century.

Society, politics and economy: Towards an industrial society, the first phase, until c. 1890

The constitutional revisions of 1840 and 1848

Constitutional revision was necessary in 1840 as a result of the independence of Belgium. Some of the leading liberals as well as progressive Roman Catholics saw a chance of introducing a number of democratic reforms. Most important of these was the introduction of ministerial responsibility. This would enable parliament to call ministers to account for the policy pursued, where formerly they reported to the King alone. Realizing that this would greatly restrict his political power, the new King, William II (1840-1848) rejected the proposed reforms. He would

An 18th-century patrician house on the Kneuterdijk in The Hague, used by King William II as a town palace in the 19th-century.

only agree to the introduction of ministerial responsibility in criminal cases.
In the following years the government was unable to reach agreement with the political leaders in favour of reform. It was only the threat of revolution such as took place in many European states in 1848, that made the King agree to a more rigorous constitutional revision.

A new constitution was proclaimed on 3 November, drafted by a committee of which the liberal leader John Rudolph Thorbecke (1798-1872) was a member. The most important amendments dealt with the way in which the Netherlands was to be administered. Ministerial responsibility to parliament was introduced, so that in principle the King could do no wrong. The Lower House, the Provincial States and municipal councils were to be elected directly by the electorate; the Upper House

would be elected by the Provincial States. The rights of amendment, interpellation and enquiry were also granted to the Lower House and it was ruled that all meetings of representative bodies were to be held in public.

Limitation of the King's power

The political power of the King had been reduced to a few well-defined rights by the constitutional revision of 1848. One of these was the right to dissolve parliament. In practice this only applied to the Lower House, with the odd exception.
King William II, could not resign himself to this restriction of his power. His son William III (1849-1890) also had difficulty in staying aloof from the parties. There was a clash of wills in 1866 when the King dissolved both Houses, because he was reluctant to accept the resignation of the government. He ordered new elections, and advised people to vote for a House which would support his team of favoured ministers. However, the King was not permitted to show partiality in this way.

At first he had his way and the cabinet stayed on. But at the first opportunity the new House expressed its disapproval of government policy. The government tendered its resignation again, and the King dissolved the House for the second time. The liberals were strongly represented in the newly-elected parliament which also expressed its disapproval of the dissolution. The King then had to admit defeat and the cabinet was sent home. A new cabinet led by the liberal Thorbecke took its place. Since then the Dutch rulers have, by and large, accepted their position as a symbol of the unity of the Dutch people, although William III continued to find this difficult. His daughter Wilhelmina, who had to succeed him in 1890 at the age of 10, did her best to comply with the constitutional rules of the game in spite of her somewhat domineering

King William II (1840-1849), by A.J. van Tetroode, 1819.

character. In the later years of her long reign, she became a true mother-figure. The period between 1840 and 1914 saw the development of the Netherlands from a predominantly agricultural society to an industrial one. In 1840, the year of William I's abdication, society was not yet in the grip of industrialization. The textile industry in Twente was underway, but there was no heavy industry to speak of. Influenced by liberal ideas, in the following years, the Netherlands economy gradually developed to become a modern capitalist economy.

In the second half of the century, Thorbecke, who was prime minister for three terms, did the most to stimulate the transition from a mercantile to a free-trade policy.

Another sign of a changing climate was the expansion of the railway network. Though the Netherlands had lagged behind in engineering in comparison with most of the industrial European countries in the early decades of the nineteenth century, the construction of railways was speeded up when the government took it in hand in 1860.

Workers unite in organizations

Industry gradually took the place of agriculture as the foremost means of support. In the second half of the century most of the manual work was taken over by machines. These developments were not beneficial to factory workers. The liberal distaste of government intervention meant that there was hardly any protection of workers' rights. When times were bad, wages were low and working hours were always long. Child labour was regarded as inevitable.

Gradually, a mood of protest grew against the inhuman conditions in which people were forced to live and work. Political groups such as the socialists undertook to help workers to speak out for themselves. They joined forces in an effort to achieve better working conditions. The Netherlands General Workers' Union was formed in 1872. This Union was against striking as a means of persuasion. This also applied to the Protestant Union, 'Patrimonium', founded in 1876 and the 'Roman Catholic Workers' Union formed by the priest Alphons Ariens.

But at the beginning of the twentieth century the argument over the right to strike was in full swing. The government attempted to stave off the possibility of a strike by passing laws prohibiting civil servants to use it as a form of protest. This led to a railway strike in 1903; but a second one, which was to be a general strike, failed when it was called for. Many workers were still unsure of their rights in this respect.

The first social legislation

For all this, the first social law was not the work of socialists or organized workers. It was the liberal member of parliament Samuel van Houten who, in 1874 introduced a bill prohibiting children under 12 years of age from working in factories. The realization was growing that the inhuman circumstances in which people toiled could not to be taken for granted. There was a government inquiry into the condition of workers in factories. Direct action followed, but the inquiry itself was a sign of the changing attitude to social problems. As a result, a number of laws were passed in the following years which led to a general improvement in the position of workers. The Factory Act was passed in 1889 prohibiting child labour and regulating working conditions for adolescent workers and women. Factory inspection was introduced to ensure that the regulations were observed. Education became compulsory in 1900; it was the implementation of this law which finally put a stop to child labour.

Emancipation of Roman Catholics

The constitution of 1848 had recognized the right to freedom of religion. The reinstatement of the Catholic hierarchy in 1853 after hundreds of years, brought furious protests from dogmatic Reformed circles; the reactions for and against that shook the nation, were known as 'the April movement'. Thorbecke's first cabinet fell on account of this affair. The emancipation of Roman Catholics took place all the same, slowly but surely.

Denominational and non-denominational
education: the battle over the schools

The right to freedom in the choice of
education was also recorded in the
constitution of 1848.
This gave rise to a struggle over financial
equality of denominational education. Until
now only non-denominational education
had been provided by the government.
A 'battle over the schools' resulted in which
the Catholics and Reformed joined in the
struggle for their own state-financed form of
education and culture. Legislation was
eventually passed in 1889 granting that the
government would also provide
denominational education.
Thorbecke also provided for a law on
secondary education in 1863, resulting in
the foundation of the so-called 'Higher
Burgher School', or H.B.S. It was to replace
the old-fashioned French school and to

H.J. Wolter, Clothing workshop in
St. Willibrordusstraat
(Historisch Museum, Amsterdam).

The Higher Burgher School in Amersfoort.

provide training geared to a modern industrial society. Like the Latin schools (known as Gymnasia since 1876), the Higher Burgher Schools were soon preparing students for a university education.

Among the socio-emancipatory movements, the women of the Netherlands could now be clearly heard in defence of a fairer society in which they would no longer be in an inferior position. Aletta Jacobs was an example to many; she was the first girl to be admitted to the H.B.S. in 1870, and she went on to complete her education at the university. She became the first woman physician in the Netherlands.

Ethical politics in relation to the colonies

The constitution of 1848 was also of great importance to the development of the Netherlands colonies. Until then the King had ruled supreme, represented by a governor general. But this power too was taken from him in 1848. This meant that a new form of government had to be set up in the Dutch East Indies. This was also introduced in the Antilles in 1865 and in Surinam where a parliament was elected in the same year.

Just as there was a growing awareness of social abuses in the Netherlands, there was also the realization that the colonies were being exploited. In 1860, the writer Edward Douwes Dekker protested under the name of 'Multatuli' ('I have suffered greatly') against the excesses of forced farming in his famous novel: 'Max Havelaar, or the coffee auctions of the Dutch Trading Company'. The outcry it caused was not in vain. The system was abolished a decade later when the Cultivation Act was adopted. This enabled farmers to lease land from the

Dutch government without the obligation of growing crops for export.

In 1899 a sensational article called 'A debt of honour' was published in an influential literary magazine called 'De Gids' (The Guide). It marked the beginning of the so-called ethical policy, favoured by those politicians who advocated a slow evolution to eventual self-rule for the colonies. But many years were to pass before this point was reached.

For a long time the Netherlands was in favour of maintaining slavery in the plantation colony of Surinam. The system was not abolished until 1863. The economy of Surinam fell into recession then in spite of the arrival of immigrant labourers from British India, and later from the Dutch East Indies, contributing to the establishment of a multi-cultural society in this West-Indian colony.

The political parties take shape

In the Netherlands political parties began to form hesitantly around 1880, as a result of industrialization, social organization and the religious-political agitation surrounding legislation on schools. The Anti-Revolutionary Party was founded in 1878 and the man behind it was Abraham Kuyper. The liberals organized themselves in the Liberal Union in 1885, on a much less rigid footing. The Roman Catholic leader Schaepman presented a political manifesto in 1883 which however was not accepted by a majority of Catholic voters until 1896. The socialists had already entered the political arena in 1888, when the Lutheran preacher Ferdinand Domela Nieuwenhuis became the first socialist to be elected to the Lower House. Domela Nieuwenhuis, who had been in prison for lese-majesty only a year before, was the leader of the Social-Democratic Union founded in 1881.

The number of men eligible to vote by law was still small between 1848 and 1887. But in 1887 the constitution was revised once more, including an electoral reform whereby everyone who could prove financial well-being and moral decency was eligible to vote. The right to vote was still reserved exclusively for men. In the eyes of socialists and radicals this reform did not go far enough; they were in favour of universal suffrage.

In 1896 the number of voters rose to more than half of the adult male population as a result of yet a new electoral law. But universal suffrage was not adopted until 1917, and even this did not include women for another two years.

King William III (1849-1890).

Vincent van Gogh (1853-1890). A rest at noon. ▼

Culture in the nineteenth century: a long-forgotten chapter

Cultural development in the Netherlands in the nineteenth century was described as complacent, provincial and unoriginal until well into the twentieth century. Nowadays we are willing to admit that there were many new developments.

Painting. The Hague School and Vincent van Gogh

After the flourishing of historical painting at the beginning of the nineteenth century, art in the Netherlands became more academic: inspiration seemed to be derived solely from traditional themes. But around 1870 a number of artists settled in The Hague who specialized in landscape and marine painting. The work of the Hague School resembled the work of French impressionists of the same period, but there was no actual connection between them. The brothers Jacob and Willem Maris are well-known representatives of the Hague School. A third brother, Matthijs, produced work akin to the symbolists, a European movement which flourished briefly at the end of the nineteenth century.
George Breitner painted true impressionistic work. His street scenes of Amsterdam are particularly expressive.

Apart from these movements the genius of Vincent van Gogh (1853-1890) was unfolding, surely the best-known Dutch artist after Rembrandt. He worked in Drenthe and Brabant at first, and later in France.

Architecture: Cuypers and Berlage

Neo-Gothic architecture came into fashion, after the 1850's, mainly prompted by the Roman Catholic emancipation. The architect Cuypers restored and designed numerous Catholic churches all over the country. He also built Amsterdam Central Station and the Rijksmuseum. This demonstrated that the emancipation was making progress; even 'national' monuments were given a 'Catholic' appearance.
Hendrik Petrus Berlage was an innovator in the Netherlands architecture. The new Amsterdam Bourse was built according to his principle that the interior parts of a building should be visible in its outward appearance, not glossed over.

Literature: the 'Men of the Eighties' and the Socialists

As the Netherlands became an ever more industrialized society, many people felt the need to escape from the anonymous, collective atmosphere which increasingly seemed to pervade life. That need was reflected in impressionistic painting but also in literature. The literary movement of the 'Men of the Eighties' which included writers and poets such as Willem Kloos and Jacques Perk, expressed an individual awareness of life, resulting in a late romantic, impressionistic view of nature. At the same time other authors and poets featured the problems of the new society in their writing; Herman Gorter and Henrietta Roland Holst were among those who expressed socialism in poetry.

◀ The Rijksmuseum, Amsterdam, one of the best known examples of 'neo' architecture by the famous architect P. Cuypers.

137

Society, politics and the economy; towards an industrial society, the second phase, c. 1890-1960

The development of a society cannot be confined between specific dates, but it is safe to state that the first phase of Dutch industrialization was completed during the last decades of the nineteenth century. In the following decades the Netherlands developed into one of the most highly-industrialized countries in the world, in spite of a lapse during the depression in the 'twenties and 'thirties.

The concept of neutrality

The threat of war could be felt all over Europe in the years before World War I broke out. The Netherlands took steps to defend itself in case of need and laws were passed in 1912 and 1913 to bring the army up to standard. However, the wish to remain neutral prevailed. General mobilization was ordered in August 1914, but this was only in order to prepare for a possible infringement of neutrality by Germany.

A neutrality crisis arose in 1916, when a British attack was expected on German-occupied Belgium. All leave was cancelled and tension mounted, until it turned out that the Germans had been mistaken in the English plans.

Pacifism and Fascism in the Netherlands between the World Wars

The Netherlands was a loyal member of the League of Nations between the two World Wars. Pacifist ideas dominated several of the political parties. Pacifism even led to constitutional revision in 1922, ruling that a declaration of war could only be made with the approval of the States General.
Most parties did not give up their pacifist ideals until a few years before World War II.

By that time their faith in a peaceful solution of conflicts had been badly shaken by developments at home.

As in the rest of Europe, a number of Fascist and semi-Fascist organizations appeared early in the 'twenties. Their members doubted whether parliamentary democracy could survive and they regarded pacifism as useless and even dangerous. One of these organizations, the National Socialist Movement (N.S.B.) joined the political arena.

Proclamation of the 'Exhibition for Peace and the League of Nations' on the Binnenhof, The Hague, 1930.

A mass demonstration held in The Hague in 1932 and organized by the Socialist Party, demanding employment measures and welfare for all.

In the 1935 elections the N.S.B. even succeeded in winning almost 8% of the votes. The Netherlands economy was at its lowest ebb in these years and it was the need of strong men, such as many people thought were in power in Germany, that caused this spectacular victory in the election. The N.S.B. was not yet particularly pro-German or anti-Semitic at that time. This came in later years when the party drifted increasingly into the German camp. The party was defeated in the elections of 1937 after which its numbers dwindled rapidly. Various anti-Fascist movements

arose, fully aware of the dangerous anti-democratic tendencies of Fascism.

Even in 1939, the impulse to avoid war was still as great as ever, but the threat of its approach could not be ignored. In August the King of Belgium and Queen Wilhelmina offered to mediate between Germany and the other European states, but general mobilization was called for in the same month. It was becoming very clear that the Netherlands would not be able to maintain neutrality this time.

The Depression during the 'thirties

The economic depression which had developed after the first World War reached its crisis in the period after 1929. The liberal view that the government should not intervene in economic affairs had to be set aside. Growing social awareness also

Colijn's crisis cabinet meets for the first time 26 May 1933. Colijn formed the so-called crisis cabinet, on a broad basis but without the Socialist Party. (SDAP)

demanded other measures than those which only promoted prosperity. Working hours had been cut in 1922; national assistance was given to the unemployed during the Depression, guaranteeing them the barest minimum income. The Ministry for Social Affairs and Employment was formed in 1933 when unemployment was high. It peaked in 1935 with over 30% of the labour force out of work.

The so-called 'Plan for Labour' was put forward in that year by the socialists, strongly rejecting liberal ideas on management. It advocated substantial government investment and a planned economy. The government succeeded in cutting unemployment figures slightly by devaluating the guilder, but there were still 300,000 people unemployed in 1939. During these difficult decades many people left the Netherlands; the United States was still the favourite destination for most emigrants.

Government policy during the Depression

The man who left his mark on government policy as prime minister in the years of crisis was Hendrik Colijn (1869-1944); he was prime minister five times between 1925 and 1939. He worked to maintain the gold standard, regarding the devaluation of the guilder as a defeat. He still won a great victory with his Anti-Revolutionary Party in the elections of 1937. In need of a strong figure, many non-Protestant voters wanted Colijn to return so that he was able to form his fourth cabinet.

The remedy which Colijn had in mind to combat the Depression was to enforce drastic economy measures. This view clashed with the Socialist Plan for Labour. Colijn could see no reason for more government investments. He attempted to bring down unemployment figures by job-creation schemes. The biggest of these projects was the reclamation of the Zuider Zee. Plans to drain this inner sea had already been made in the nineteenth century, but these had been rejected. In 1892 a project designed by the engineer C. Lely (1854-1929) was approved by a government committee. This gigantic task was not begun until 1918 when Lely himself was Minister for Public Works and his bill for the partial reclamation of the Zuider Zee was passed. Once the Wieringermeer polder had been drained in 1930, the Zuider Zee was permanently enclosed by the IJsselmeer Dam, completed in 1933. Reclamation of the Northeast polder was already in progress, but this was held up in the second half of the 'thirties due to the lack of funds.

Multinationals

There were some favourable economic developments in spite of so much social misery. The rich sources of raw materials in the Dutch East Indies, and later the strong position of the Netherlands trade and industry on the international market combined to promote the establishment and growth of companies which soon became multinationals. The Royal Dutch Petroleum Company which later merged with the English Shell, and in the 'twenties and 'thirties Philips, are examples of this. There were also some modern companies winning international recognition by regulating water control in the Dutch tradition.

Head Office of the Royal Netherlands Petroleum Company in The Hague, built between 1915 and 1917 in neo 16th-century renaissance style. The company later merged with the English Shell Oil Company.

The interior of the 'Concertgebouw' of Amsterdam, completed in 1888.

Culture in the period between the two World Wars

A new movement in the visual arts: 'The Style'

Among the many developments in the arts following the First World War there was an interesting movement called 'The Style' which attracted international attention. It was called after a journal which first appeared in 1917; the founders of The Style represented various forms of art. For instance, Theo van Doesburg and Piet Mondriaan painted, J.J.P. Oud was an architect. The keynote of The Style was to strip art of every unnecessary detail. In architecture this meant that buildings were starkly functional, their structure outlined visibly and without any ornamentation where possible. The most handsome example of this is perhaps the Schröder House in Utrecht, a private house designed by Gerrit Rietveld in 1924 and now open to the public.

Literature

The same moralism seen in visual arts was also found in literature. Writers such as Slauerhoff, Ter Braak and Du Perron wanted to uphold and pass on the essence and the best in the tradition of the Netherlands by stripping it of false ornament and sentiment. The poets Bloem and Nijhoff were less controversial, but all writers, poets, artists and architects were aware that this was a time for reflection. The disaster of World War I had demonstrated that Europe was ill-served by carrying on the old traditions without question.

Music

In music too, there was much going on. Composers such as Pijper and Andriessen left their marks. Also the Concertgebouw Orchestra won increasing fame both at home and abroad. During the entire twentieth century, the Concertgebouw Orchestra has continued to hold a reputation for magnificent performances of contemporary music by composers such as Ravel, Stravinski and Mahler who was a great friend of the Orchestra's famous conductor during the 'twenties, Willem Mengelberg.

The mass media

The new mass media- film, radio and gramophone - made their entry during the first decades of the twentieth century. They soon revolutionized Dutch cultural life. Three of the broadcasting corporations operating today were already in action in 1925. Most families in the 'thirties owned a wireless set. They were able to listen to (world) news bulletins, sports commentaries, popular and classical music, formerly beyond the means of most, and radio plays, which soon became highly popular.
Each broadcasting corporation represented a specific religious denomination or ideology, showing that the 'pillarization' of the Netherlands society, in groups with their own religious identity, also pervaded culture.

Science

The Netherlands' leading position as an industrial nation was also reflected in great progress in science and engineering. The laboratories of the universities of Leiden and Amsterdam produced many Nobel prizewinners in the first decades of the twentieth century. In physics and astronomy, Lorentz, Kamerlingh Onnes, Van der Waals and Kapteyn had a world-wide reputation.

143

A squad of the SS. Battalion of guards North-West, formed 1 January 1942 by order of Heinrich Himmler. The 1st company was detailed to guard Camp Amersfoort.

Society and politics during World War II

The German occupation: 1940-1945

German troops invaded the Netherlands on 10th May 1940. This marked the end of a period of peace which had lasted for over a century. The country had managed to stay out of international conflicts since the struggle with Belgium in 1839 ended with its separation from the Kingdom of the Netherlands. But now neutrality could no longer be maintained.
After several days of fierce fighting it was clear that the poorly-equipped Dutch army could not hold out against the superior strength of the Germans. Queen Wilhelmina and her Ministers left for England unhindered on 13th May, after foiling German plans to take them prisoner.
A catastrophic bombardment of Rotterdam and Middelburg followed; when the Germans threatened to destroy other towns if the struggle was prolonged, army command was forced to capitulate on 15th May. (Zeeland on the 17th of May).

Persecution of the Jews

Arthur Seyss-Inquart took up his position as Reich Commissioner on 29th May. It was soon clear that the anti-Semitism displayed by the German government would also be flaunted in the Netherlands. In October 1940 all civil servants had to produce a declaration of Aryan origin. The majority of the population did not yet realize the extent of German anti-Semitism so that many of the declarations were signed.

Any hopes that the Jews in this country would not be persecuted were dashed in July 1942. The first groups of Jewish people were transported to extermination camps, under the pretext of employment projects in Germany and Poland. In a little over a year

100,000 Jews had been wiped out in this way; the Jewish population of the Netherlands was decimated. Only a few escaped deportation by going into hiding with Dutch families.

The first resistance organizations were formed at an early stage. They were to play an important part for the duration of the war in espionage activities and in helping those who, like the Jews soon realized they had to go into hiding; above all they helped to keep up the morale of the Dutch people. Queen Wilhelmina made her own contribution in this respect by encouraging her people in Radio Orange broadcasts from London. As a result, the Royal family became a symbol of freedom.

The liberation of the Netherlands: 1944 and 1945

The allied armies - including Dutch units - landed in Normandy on 6th June 1944; this was followed by "Mad Tuesday" in the Netherlands on 5th September. It was started by a rumour that parts of the country had already been liberated by allied troops; the rumour was so strong that German troops and numerous members of the N.S.B. left for the eastern frontier.
But another winter passed before the whole of the Netherlands was liberated, a winter of famine. All means of transport had been requisitioned by the Germans so that distribution came to a standstill; the result was a shortage of food everywhere.
When part of the Netherlands was liberated on 29th April 1945, the first of a series of food parcels was dropped by air and greatly appreciated by the starving population.

The war ended on 5th May when the Germans signed the capitulation in the presence of Prince Bernhard, the husband of crown princess Juliana, who represented the Netherlands. He had assumed command of the so-called Domestic Force in September 1944; this was a military umbrella organization for all the different resistance groups, which often fought amongst themselves.

The return of the Royal Family was a sign to all that the war was really over.

Queen Wilhelmina and Princess Juliana, the House of Orange personified after their return from exile.

Society, politics, and economy after 1945: reconstruction

Post-war housing.

Clearing the rubble and starting again: new politics and parties

In the first post-war years the various cabinets could not do much more than to clear away the rubble, quite literally. However, during the war ideas had been born and discussed in various sociopolitical circles, in the hope of altering the social structure to solve some of the worst problems. This meant that some pre-war situations did not recur. For example, council housing ensured that people with a low income could also live in homes with modern conveniences. Of course this was not achieved in a day, and the housing shortage went on for a very long time. There were also some political parties which did not return after the war. Other parties took their places, based on the old ideals of liberalism and socialism, but better adapted to the realities of post-war life. These included the Labour Party (PVDA), formed in 1946, the Peoples' Party for Freedom and Democracy (VVD) formed in 1948 and the Catholic Peoples' Party (KVP), also formed after the war.

Two pre-war parties which did return were those based on Protestant principles: the Christian Historical Union and the Anti-Revolutionary Party. These two parties merged with the KVP to form the present Christian Democratic Appel (CDA) in 1976.

Participation in international consultation

Good progress was made in international co-operation after the war. The wish to join international consultative bodies was strong in the Netherlands, for the very reason that it is a small country. It was a member of the United Nations from the start in 1945. A customs union was formed with Belgium and Luxembourg in 1944, which was consolidated in the Benelux in 1948. The Netherlands has also belonged to the NATO from the first. The European Community has always had the wholehearted support of the Dutch, in the hope that their ideals regarding society would be upheld and strengthened, especially by the advantages of economic and political co-operation.

The Dutch East Indies declares its independence: Indonesia is born

The colonies - which had been renamed 'overseas territories' in the constitutional revision of 1922 - became independent, or partially so, after the war. In the case of the Dutch East Indies this was preceded by an unsuccessful Dutch military campaign.

Some indigenous political parties had declared the independence of Indonesia immediately after the capitulation of Japan, which had occupied the Dutch East Indies for almost four years. The Netherlands government then considered granting independence to 'the United States of Indonesia', but within the kingdom. An agreement to this effect was signed between the Netherlands and the Republic of Indonesia at Linnadjati in 1946. The Republic, which dominated Sumatra and Java, wanted to extend its powers to the other parts of the archipelago, which did not welcome this development. In the ensuing confusion, the first 'police action' was carried out by the Dutch government in 1947, when Dutch troops tried to protect the interests of these other regions. After a second campaign in 1949, a round-table conference was held at The Hague; the transfer of sovereignty took place on 27 December of that year, whereby the Republic of Indonesia gained command of the whole archipelago.

The Charter of the Kingdom is granted to the former colonies in the West

There had already been a round-table conference between the Netherlands, Surinam and the Netherlands Antilles in 1948. After a third conference in 1954, the Charter of the Kingdom was declared, granting the overseas territories in the West far-reaching independence. Surinam became autonomous in 1975. A suitable form of sovereignty, acceptable to all the islands of the Netherlands Antilles is still under consideration.

The European Parliament at Straatsburg

Society, politics and economy after 1960

The House of Orange

The post-war period in the Netherlands was a disappointment to Queen Wilhelmina. During the war she had developed various ideas concerning an ideal society. But the confusing reality of politics in the aftermath of war did not live up to this. She abdicated in favour of her daughter Juliana when she celebrated her fiftieth jubilee in 1948.

The place of the sovereign is still filled by a member of the House of Orange. Queen Juliana in her turn abdicated in favour of her eldest daughter in 1980, since when Queen Beatrix has symbolized the unity of the people of the Netherlands in her own way.

The Delta project accomplished

A great deal of work has been done in civil engineering. Many motorways have been built and the Zuider Zee project was continued with the reclamation of eastern and southern Flevoland. The debate concerning the reclamation of the western part known as Markerwaard is still going on.
The Delta project has also been realized. The plan was drafted as a result of a disastrous storm which flooded the islands of Zeeland in 1953, at the cost of 1835 lives. The project protects the low-lying areas of the southwestern Netherlands from the dangers of flooding. A start was made in 1957 when all the Zeeland inlets were sealed off. The storm-surge barrier in the Eastern Scheldt was brought into operation by Queen Beatrix in 1986. This gigantic feat of

engineering had taken almost thirty years to complete; together with the Zuider Zee project, it established the Netherlands worldwide reputation in this field.

Economic boom and recession; social legislation and social problems

After the war, many people tired of waiting for the economy to recover and decided to emigrate. At the beginning of the 'fifties hundreds of thousands of people left the country, and this time their destination was either Australia, Canada or New Zealand. In the same period a wave of immigrants arrived from the Dutch East Indies, to be followed later by a steady stream of people from Surinam and the Antilles; there were over 400,000 of them altogether.

Meanwhile, there was work to be done in the Netherlands. Food rationing was lifted in 1949 and there were several rounds of wage increases of 5% at a time to raise the standard of living. This policy, coupled with fresh investments, expanding industries and strongly increasing exports, boosted the economy towards the end of the 'fifties. As a result, the Netherlands economy, though prospering, became highly sensitive to fluctuations in the international economy. There was something of a boom in the 'sixties, partly due to membership of the European Economic Community which the Netherlands joined in 1957. This continued until well into the 'seventies when the international economic crisis also made itself felt in this country.

◀ *Portrait of Queen Beatrix on the occasion of her coronation in 1980 (Public Information Service R.V.D. The Hague).*

The Eastern Scheldt storm-surge barrier is part of the Delta project to safeguard the islands of Zeeland against the water. ▶

The greatest post-war politician was probably Dr. Willem Drees (1886 -1988). He was Minister for Social Affairs in the first two post-war cabinets; in that period he provided for the old-age pension, by special legislation. He went on to lead four coalitions representing all the big parties between 1948 and 1958. The social security system, forming the basis of the much-admired and much-maligned Netherlands welfare state, has its roots in this period. The system was not put to the test during the years of affluence. Unemployment figures had fallen so sharply that it was considered necessary to take in immigrant labourers from Italy, Greece, Spain and later also from Morocco and Turkey. Many of these workers settled permanently in the Netherlands. The independence of the overseas territories after World War II also led to the wave of immigrants mentioned above, especially from Surinam and the Antilles in the 'seventies and 'eighties. These two waves of immigrants have made the Netherlands multicultural in the extreme. The government enables all minority groups to uphold their own cultural values, but it is also essential that the groups concerned are assimilated in the Netherlands society and culture. Constitutional revision has since granted foreign workers in this country the right to take part in municipal elections.

However, the social security system has been put to the test due to the decline in the economy since the 'eighties; this has led to social and political tension.
During the period of affluence between 1960 and 1974 there was a tendency to look for new ideals, especially among the young. Now their efforts are once more concentrated on ordering their lives and futures as comfortably as possible. Employment is in short supply, and social services have less to offer so that the average Dutch person is intent on finding and holding down a job. This leaves little

time for excessive social criticism and this is also reflected in foreign policy. In the 'sixties and 'seventies, many of the Dutch could see no sense in the arms race and various huge protest demonstrations were held to express their revulsion against the use of nuclear weapons. This pacifist attitude sometimes became anti-American, particularly among leftists. There have been less signs of this since the disarmament talks were held between Russia and America and especially since the fall of communism in Eastern Europe in 1989 and 1990. Involvement with the serious problems facing society seems to have grown less intense during the 'eighties, probably due to individual concern over economic well-being.

Society and culture after 1960

Education in the Netherlands has been entirely re-organized since the war, starting with the 'Mammoth Act' on secondary education under Minister Cals; this was passed in 1963 and implemented in 1968. This Act was to promote streaming from one type of education to another, especially for the benefit of social groups which would formerly not have felt able to enter higher education. The Primary Education Act implemented in 1985 did away with the distinction between the infant and primary schools, bringing the school age down to 5 years. The re-organization of higher education in the 'eighties led to cuts in the length of university studies, and mergers between the various forms of vocational training.

One of the creative post-war movements in the Netherlands - the abstract art produced by members of the Cobra group - became internationally famous. Karel Appel was the best-known artist of this group.
In literature the 'Men of the Fifties' included Lucebert and Remco Campert, who wrote experimental poetry. The writer Van 't Reve also broke with tradition in his work.

It is a fact that after the Second World War there was a general longing for a breakthrough to more freedom in the various forms of expression, unhampered by a tradition that according to many only led to a fiasco. Was not this the lesson World War II had taught? These feelings seem reminiscent of the mood in the period after World War I.

The natural sequence of this development now is that the barriers between the traditional socio-religious 'compartments' or 'pillars' are breaking down; culture and society cannot be kept within the confines of religious and ideological subgroups any longer. But the loss of tradition and the socio-cultural framework, which used to provide a sense of security, sometimes seems to make people long for the old ideas and movements of the past.

The multifunctional 'Facilities building' of Leiden University. Designed in the 'eighties, it is an example of modern Dutch architecture.

Conclusion

It would not do to end a historical survey with predictions for the future. But it seems fitting to point out that generally speaking, the Netherlands and the Dutch people during the last years of the twentieth century, seem to have a clearly-defined idea of their own culture and society. Formed in the past, this self-knowledge serves as a guideline for life in the present, on the eve of the year 2000, and may do so too, for the unforeseeable future.

A small nation which likes to think it is both tolerant and cosmopolitan. The coming decades will reveal whether this is true.

A small country which is apt to boast from time to time. Won from the water, formerly one of the leading commercial powers in the world, it is still one of its most highly industrialized societies. It has also endeavoured to attain a high standard of social justice. The coming decades will reveal whether these achievements can stand the test of time.

A small state which is prepared to relinquish some of the traditional elements of sovereignty and independence to promote welfare and well-being in a broader setting. The coming decades will reveal whether this policy bears fruit.

In short, the Netherlands likes to take the lead in Europe and the world. This incurs both admiration and irritation, because as a nation, it remains 'small among the great'.

The 'Westertoren' in Amsterdam bearing the Emperor's crown, a privilege granted to the city in 1489 by Maximilian of Austria. ▶

CHRONOLOGICAL OUTLINE

57 B.C.		Prehistory
	c. 10,000 B.C.	The last ice ages
	c. 1900-750 B.C.	The bronze age
	c. 750 B.C.	The iron age
57 B.C. - A.D. 406		Roman rule
until c. 650		Germanic society Saxons, Frisians, Franks. Conversion to Christianity
c. 650 - 850		The Carolingian Empire
	800-814	Charlemagne
c. 850 - 1000		The Norsemen
c. 1000		The development of territorial principalitie Regional sovereignty
c. 1200		The towns set the tone in politics, economy and culture
1350 - 1581		Burgundian-Hapsburg rule. Centralization of power and authority The Reformation
	1515-1555	Charles V
	1555-1581	Philip II
1586 - 1648		The 'Eighty Years' War'; Rebellion against foreign rule
	1576	The Pacification of Ghent
	1579	The Union of Atrecht and the Union of Utrecht
1581		The Act of Abjuration
1581		Establishment of 'The Republic of the Seven United Provinces'
1648		The Peace of Münster; recognition of the Republic

17th century		The Golden Age. Voyages of discovery. Establishment of United East India Company and West India Company
18th century	1747	The Republic a second-rate power. Oranges stadhouders by inheritance Patriots and Orangists
1795 - 1806		The Batavian Republic
1806 - 1810		King Louis Napoleon
1810 - 1813		The French Period
1814 - 1830/39		The Kingdom of the United Netherlands
	1814-1840	King William I
	1830	Establishment of the Belgian State
1839		The Kingdom of the Netherlands
	1840-1849	King William II
	1849-1890	King William III
	1890-1948	Queen Wilhelmina
	1948-1980	Queen Juliana
	1980	Queen Beatrix
	1840 and 1848	Constitutional revisions
1840 - 1890		Towards an industrial society; phase one
1890 - 1945		Towards an industrial society; phase two
	1914-1940	Policy of neutrality. Pacifism - Fascism. Economic crisis
	1940-1945	The German occupation during World War II
1945 - 1960		Reconstruction. Participation in international consultation
1960		Economic boom and recession

Simplified family tree of the House of Orange-Nassau

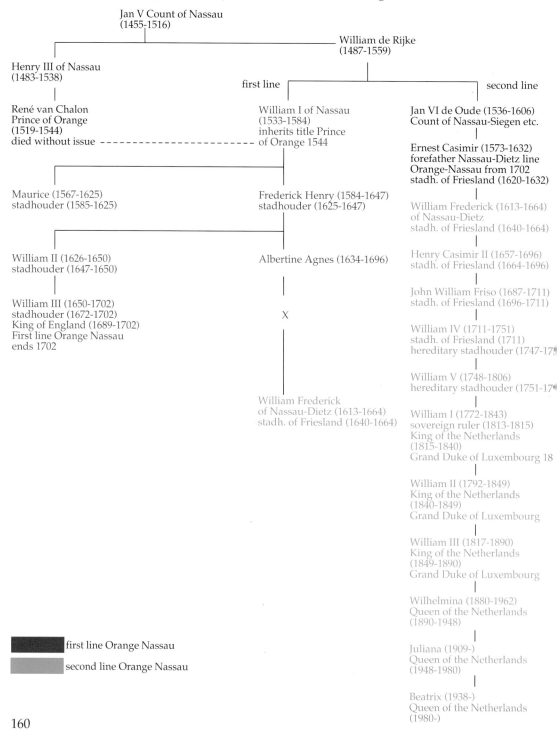

Jan V Count of Nassau
(1455-1516)

William de Rijke
(1487-1559)

Henry III of Nassau
(1483-1538)

first line

second line

René van Chalon
Prince of Orange
(1519-1544)
died without issue -

William I of Nassau
(1533-1584)
inherits title Prince
of Orange 1544

Jan VI de Oude (1536-1606)
Count of Nassau-Siegen etc.

Ernest Casimir (1573-1632)
forefather Nassau-Dietz line
Orange-Nassau from 1702
stadh. of Friesland (1620-1632)

Maurice (1567-1625)
stadhouder (1585-1625)

Frederick Henry (1584-1647)
stadhouder (1625-1647)

William Frederick (1613-1664)
of Nassau-Dietz
stadh. of Friesland (1640-1664)

William II (1626-1650)
stadhouder (1647-1650)

Albertine Agnes (1634-1696)

Henry Casimir II (1657-1696)
stadh. of Friesland (1664-1696)

William III (1650-1702)
stadhouder (1672-1702)
King of England (1689-1702)
First line Orange Nassau
ends 1702

X

John William Friso (1687-1711)
stadh. of Friesland (1696-1711)

William IV (1711-1751)
stadh. of Friesland (1711)
hereditary stadhouder (1747-17▮)

William V (1748-1806)
hereditary stadhouder (1751-17▮)

William Frederick
of Nassau-Dietz (1613-1664)
stadh. of Friesland (1640-1664)

William I (1772-1843)
sovereign ruler (1813-1815)
King of the Netherlands
(1815-1840)
Grand Duke of Luxembourg 18

William II (1792-1849)
King of the Netherlands
(1840-1849)
Grand Duke of Luxembourg

William III (1817-1890)
King of the Netherlands
(1849-1890)
Grand Duke of Luxembourg

Wilhelmina (1880-1962)
Queen of the Netherlands
(1890-1948)

Juliana (1909-)
Queen of the Netherlands
(1948-1980)

Beatrix (1938-)
Queen of the Netherlands
(1980-)

first line Orange Nassau

second line Orange Nassau